GEOLOGICAL SCIENCES

GEOLOGICAL SCIENCES

EDITED BY JOHN P. RAFFERTY, ASSOCIATE EDITOR,
EARTH AND LIFE SCIENCES

Britannica®
Educational Publishing

IN ASSOCIATION WITH

ROSEN
EDUCATIONAL SERVICES

Published in 2012 by Britannica Educational Publishing
(a trademark of Encyclopædia Britannica, Inc.)
in association with Rosen Educational Services, LLC
29 East 21st Street, New York, NY 10010.

First Edition

Britannica Educational Publishing
Michael I. Levy: Executive Editor
J.E. Luebering: Senior Manager
Marilyn L. Barton: Senior Coordinator, Production Control
Steven Bosco: Director, Editorial Technologies
Lisa S. Braucher: Senior Producer and Data Editor
Yvette Charboneau: Senior Copy Editor
Kathy Nakamura: Manager, Media Acquisition
John P. Rafferty: Associate Editor, Earth and Life Sciences

Rosen Educational Services
Jeanne Nagle: Senior Editor
Nelson Sá: Art Director
Cindy Reiman: Photography Manager
Matthew Cauli: Designer, Cover Design
Introduction by John P. Rafferty

Library of Congress Cataloging-in-Publication Data

Geological sciences/edited by John P. Rafferty. — 1st ed.
   p. cm. — (Geology: landforms, minerals, and rocks)
"In association with Britannica Educational Publishing, Rosen Educational Services."
Includes bibliographical references and index.
ISBN 978-1-61530-495-0 (library binding)
1. Geology. I. Rafferty, John P.
QE28.G323 2012
550—dc22

                                                                    2010047139

Manufactured in the United States of America

On the cover (front and back): Geological layers, grave, Petra, Jordan. *Patrice Hauser/ Photographer's Choice/Getty Images*
On the cover (front top), p. 1: Stalagtites and stalagmites in an illuminated cave (far left); paleontologists chip at a rock face in Madagascar (second from left); geologic folds at a cliff face in Spain (second from right); a geologist works with a pickaxe to dislodge samples (far right). *Shutterstock.com; Maria Stenzel/National Geographic Image Collection/Getty Images; Shutterstock.com; Shutterstock.com*

On pages 1, 37, 99, 129, 192, 194, 199: Dinosaur fossils found in Alberta, Canada. *AbleStock/ Jupiterimages*

CONTENTS

42

50

73

92

100

122

151

175

188

INTRODUCTION

The Earth sciences are a collection of disciplines that consider Earth's atmosphere and hydrosphere, as well as the planet's solid aspect, the geosphere. The academic disciplines concerned with the geosphere are collectively called the geological sciences, or geosciences. Each one considers different facets of Earth's surface and interior, such as its rocks, minerals, and their chemistry, the evolution and role of its landforms, and its geologic history. Although most of the geosciences exist to develop a greater understanding of the parts and processes involved in the solid Earth, the subfield of economic geology takes as its mission the extraction of rocks and minerals and their conversion to useful products.

This book initiates readers into the study of geology and the rest of the geological sciences. Along the way, readers will meet many of the explorers and thinkers that plumbed the geosphere and laid the foundations of geologic study, learning about their contributions and virtually examining some of the tools they used to draw their conclusions.

The work of modern geoscientists is the direct result of knowledge gained from thousands of years of observation and investigation. Initial forays into the geological sciences, which likely occurred before written records were kept, probably involved the collection of useful stones and gems, as well as observances of earthquakes and volcanic activity. The ancient Greeks and the Chinese were the first to record geological phenomena, seeing fossils as forms of ancient life and clues to environments of the past rather than as simple curiosities.

Major advances in the study of geology, however, did not occur until the 1500s and later. During this period, the

Geologists at work in Chile's La Escondida mine. Keith Wood/The Image Bank/Getty Images

basic tenets of stratigraphy, which is the study and classification of rock layers, were put forth. In the late 1660s, Danish scientist and theologian Nicolaus Steno developed the principle of superposition, which states that younger layers of rock rest above older layers.

Other developments followed. Scottish scientist James Hutton described the concept of uniformitarianism, which maintains that the geologic processes that take place in the present also occurred in the past. Thus, past geologic events, such as the changes in ancient river basins, could be explained by processes that were still occurring today. In the early 19th century, the work of French scientist René-Just Haüy concerning minerals and their crystal features produced the science of crystallography. In 1837 Louis Agassiz, a Swiss-born scientist and teacher from the United States, posited that the placement of large boulders far from their points of origin resulted from the movements of tremendous ice sheets.

In 1905, the first steps toward developing radiometric dating, a technique designed to calculate the approximate age of a rock or mineral, were made by American chemist Bertram Boltwood. Noting that the shape of the western coast of Africa could theoretically fit together with the eastern coast of South America, German meteorologist Alfred Wegener proposed the theory of continental drift in 1912. Wegener's theory held that continents were not stationary, but, rather, that they moved to new positions across vast intervals of geologic time.

A watershed moment in the development of the geological sciences occurred in the 1960s. Scientists from the United States and the United Kingdom uncovered evidence that new oceanic crust formed along the mid-oceanic ridges, a long chain of underwater mountains that occur at the boundaries between Earth's tectonic plates, and that these ridges were spreading. Rocks in the new crust also recorded periodic reversals of Earth's magnetic field. This new information enabled scientists to develop a driving mechanism for Wegener's theory and better explain the dynamics of several other geologic processes, such as volcanic eruptions and rock folding.

Today, the jumping-off point for the modern study of the geologic sciences is geology, which is the discipline concerned with Earth, the materials that form it, and the various chemical reactions and physical forces that act upon the planet's surface and its interior. At the heart of geology is mineralogy, the subdiscipline that focuses on the classification of minerals and the study of their characteristics and behavior. Minerals are the basic components of rocks. They are naturally occurring solids containing unique crystalline geometries that reflect their unique chemical structures. The study of a mineral's geometric properties and internal structure fall within the purview of crystallography, whereas the study of its chemical structure, as well as that of the rock that contains it, falls to the subdiscipline of geochemistry.

Mineralogists, petrologists (scientists who study rocks), crystallographers, and geochemists are only a fraction of the people working within the geosciences. Geodesists, geophysicists, and structural geologists consider Earth's structure beyond the scale of individual rocks and minerals. The science of geodesy investigates Earth's size and shape and provides the means, through a series of surveyed points on the surface, to create maps of Earth's features. Such maps and reference points may be used by other geoscientists to frame their own investigations.

Geophysics is a wide-ranging discipline concerned with changes to Earth's gravitational field, the movement of seismic waves and electricity through Earth's crust and interior, and the role Earth's magnetic field plays on the planet's geology. This science also considers how Earth's magnetic field behaves when it is exposed to different types of external radiation, the transmission of heat from the planet's interior, and how all of these factors interact with one another.

Similarly, structural geology covers a wide area. This subdiscipline spans everything from the imperfections within a given mineral crystal to the forces that shape mountains and Earth's tectonic plates. Another subdiscipline, tectonics, strives to make comprehensible how the planet formed and how it continues to evolve, whereas volcanology seeks to understand the behaviour of volcanoes and their contributions to Earth's crust.

Other subdisciplines of geology focus exclusively on Earth's surface features and the forces that alter them. Geomorphology attempts to understand the processes that create and destroy landforms. For example, fluvial geomorphologists—that is, those that examine the forces and processes that occur in river systems—study how the movement of water affects the various landforms that occur within watersheds, as well as those landscape features (river banks, streambeds) that appear within the river itself. Water is also the focus of glacial geology, but only when this ubiquitous compound occurs as ice. This particular subdivision examines the behaviour of ice and how its movement can create, destroy, and modify Earth's surface features.

Geologists also seek to establish a timeline of major events in Earth's history, such as the movements of continents, the evolution of life, the colonization of the land by trees, and the timing of mass extinctions. Earth's history, which spans approximately 4.5 billion years, is far longer than recorded human history, so geologists look for clues in rocks. One of the aforementioned principles of geology states that, in general, the layers of sedimentary rock get older the deeper one digs. The order of the rock layers can provide the geologist with a sense of the sequencing of specific geologic events. In addition, the absolute age of some rocks can be determined by examining the decay of the radioactive isotopes contained therein.

Other clues can be found in the fossilized remains of certain organisms. Some fossils, called index fossils, have tremendously large distributions that span multiple continents. They can be used to assist in understanding the relative age of a rock, the environmental conditions present when the rock was formed, and the orientation of the different landmasses upon which the rock was discovered.

The examination of fossils falls within the purview of paleontology. Paleontologists are scientists who study extinct life. The field is divided up into three parts: invertebrate paleontology, which generally focuses on fossil invertebrates from marine environments; vertebrate paleontology, which examines fossil animals with backbones; and micropaleontology, which investigates fossil zooplankton, such as tiny crustaceans and foraminifera. Fossil plants, which include different types of algae, also are helpful in establishing the timeline of geologic events. Paleobotany is the field concerned with their study, whereas the study of pollen, spores, and very tiny planktonic organisms is considered within the broad field of palynology.

Geology is not necessarily restricted to Earth. Other planets and solid bodies in the solar system and beyond are composed of rock. The geology of some of these worlds may be affected by the same forces that appear on Earth, or they may be the product of utterly alien conditions, for example, their proximity to the local star or their orbit.

The study of the geology in worlds beyond our own is called astrogeology.

One of the most important subdisciplines of geology, in that it affects the lives of most human beings on a daily basis, is economic geology. Modern civilization cannot function without materials extracted from the solid Earth. The development of techniques to find and recover petroleum from between deep layers of rock is probably one of this field's most important activities. Fuel oil for heating and gasoline and diesel fuel for transportation are some of the world's most valuable products. Along with coal and natural gas, petroleum-derived fuels—often referred to as fossil fuels--keep automobiles and other vehicles moving and electricity flowing. Without these services, the economies of many societies would grind to a halt. Thousands of other products, in addition to fuels, are made from petroleum. Plastics, synthetic rubbers and fabrics, cosmetics, road tar, and waxes are all made from this material. Petroleum derivatives are even used in foods and medicines.

The fruits of economic geology also extend to other industries. In many areas around the world, soils must be stabilized with sand, gravel, and rock to prevent the collapse or degradation of buildings that are constructed upon them. Additionally, many of the materials used to build houses and other structures are extracted from the ground. Limestone and clay are ingredients in cement used to create a structure's foundation, sheets of drywall made of gypsum often separate interior spaces, and copper is used to make electrical wiring. Other metals recovered from the solid Earth are used to make nails, screws, reinforcing bars in concrete (rebar), joints, pipes, and parts of the ventilation system. In addition, the extraction of precious minerals (such as diamonds, rubies, and sapphires from corundum, and emeralds from beryl) and precious ores such as gold, silver, and platinum supports more than just the jewelry industry. Many of these materials are used to build tools for industrial processes or parts for electronic devices.

The geological sciences make up an important aspect of the Earth sciences. They are a collection of disciplines that contribute greatly to the understanding of the materials that make up the solid Earth and the structure of the planet's interior. Some of these disciplines—most notably geochemistry, geophysics, and paleontology—employ the tools and techniques of the other sciences in order to discover and explain geological phenomena. As new technologies with which to study the solid Earth emerge, teams of different specialists from the geosciences and other fields will continue to collaborate with one another to unlock the mysteries of the planet.

CHAPTER 1
EVOLUTION OF THE GEOLOGIC SCIENCES

The Earth sciences are made up of the fields of study concerned with the solid Earth, its waters, and the air that envelops it. The broad aim of the Earth sciences is to understand the present features and the past evolution of Earth and to use this knowledge, where appropriate, for the benefit of humankind. Thus the basic concerns of the Earth scientist are to observe, describe, and classify all the features of Earth, whether characteristic or not, in order to generate hypotheses with which to explain their presence and development. Earth scientists also devise means of checking opposing ideas for their relative validity. In this way the most plausible, acceptable, and long-lasting ideas are developed.

The geologic sciences constitute one division of the Earth sciences. Geology and its related subfields focus on the phenomena occurring within the planet or on its surface. The Earth sciences also include the hydrologic and atmospheric sciences.

It is worth emphasizing two important features that the geological sciences have in common with the other two divisions of the Earth sciences. First is the inaccessibility of many of the objects of study. Many rocks, as well as water and oil reservoirs, are at great depths in Earth, while air masses circulate at vast heights above it. Second, there is the fourth dimension—time. Geological scientists are responsible for working out how Earth evolved over millions of years. For example, what were the physical and

THE DIVISION OF EARTH SCIENCES

Today the Earth sciences are divided into many disciplines, which are themselves divisible into six groups. Although a few of the disciplines listed below fall within the scope of the hydrologic and atmospheric sciences, the majority relate directly to the science of geology and its related subdisciplines.

1. Those subjects that deal with the water and air at or above the solid surface of Earth. These include the study of the water on and within the ground (hydrology), glaciers and ice caps (glaciology), oceans (oceanography), the atmosphere and its phenomena (meteorology), and world climates (climatology). Such fields of study are grouped under the hydrologic and atmospheric sciences and are treated separately from the geologic sciences, which focus on the solid Earth.

2. Disciplines concerned with the physical-chemical makeup of the solid Earth, which include the study of minerals (mineralogy), the three main groups of rocks (igneous, sedimentary, and metamorphic petrology), the chemistry of rocks (geochemistry), the structures in rocks (structural geology), and the physical properties of rocks on Earth's surface and within its interior (geophysics).

3. The study of landforms (geomorphology), which is concerned with the description of the features of the present terrestrial surface and an analysis of the processes that gave rise to them.

4. Disciplines concerned with Earth's geologic history, including the study of fossils and the fossil record (paleontology), the development of sedimentary strata deposited typically over millions of years (stratigraphy), and the isotopic chemistry and age dating of rocks (geochronology).

5. Applied Earth sciences dealing with current practical applications beneficial to society. These include the study of fossil fuels (oil, natural gas, and coal); oil reservoirs; mineral deposits; geothermal energy for electricity and heating; the structure and composition of bedrock for the location of

bridges, nuclear reactors, roads, dams, and skyscrapers and other buildings; hazards involving rock and mud avalanches, volcanic eruptions, earthquakes, and the collapse of tunnels; and coastal, cliff, and soil erosion.

6. The study of the rock record on the Moon, the planets, and their satellites (astrogeology). This field includes the investigation of relevant terrestrial features—namely, tektites (glassy objects resulting from meteorite impacts) and astroblemes (meteorite craters).

With such intergradational boundaries between the divisions of the Earth sciences—which, on a broader scale, also overlap with physics, chemistry, biology, mathematics, and certain branches of engineering—researchers today must be versatile in their approach to problems.

chemical conditions operating on Earth and the Moon 3.5 billion years ago? How did the oceans and atmosphere form, and how did their chemical composition change with time? How did life begin, and how has life evolved?

ORIGINS IN PREHISTORIC TIMES

The origins of the geological sciences lie in the myths and legends of the distant past. The creation story, which can be traced to a Babylonian epic of the 22nd century BCE and is told in the first chapter of Genesis in the bible, has proved most influential. The story is cast in the form of Earth history and thus was readily accepted as an embodiment of scientific as well as of theological truth.

Earth scientists later made innumerable observations of natural phenomena and interpreted them in an increasingly multidisciplinary manner. The geological and other

Earth sciences, however, were slow to develop largely because the progress of science was constrained by whatever society would tolerate or support at any one time.

ANTIQUITY

Humans likely studied Earth's structure, composition, and geologic history since before the dawn of writing. The Greeks and the Chinese were among the first peoples to record their observations. Despite limited technology, geological scientists of the time made the first attempts to classify and describe different planetary phenomena.

KNOWLEDGE OF EARTH COMPOSITION AND STRUCTURE

The oldest known treatise on rocks and minerals is the *De lapidibus* ("On Stones") of the Greek philosopher Theophrastus(*c.* 372–*c.* 287 BCE). Written probably in the early years of the 3rd century, this work remained the best study of mineral substances for almost 2,000 years. Although reference is made to some 70 different materials, the work is more an effort at classification than systematic description.

In early Chinese writings on mineralogy, stones and rocks were distinguished from metals and alloys, and further distinctions were made on the basis of colour and other physical properties. The speculations of Zheng Sixiao (died 1332 CE) on the origin of ore deposits were more advanced than those of his contemporaries in Europe. In brief, his theory was that ore is deposited from groundwater circulating in subsurface fissures.

Ancient accounts of earthquakes and volcanic eruptions are sometimes valuable as historical records but tell little about the causes of these events. Aristotle (384–322

BCE) and Strabo (64 BCE–c. 21 CE) held that volcanic explosions and earthquakes alike are caused by spasmodic motions of hot winds that move underground and occasionally burst forth in volcanic activity attended by Earth tremors. Classical and medieval ideas on earthquakes and volcanoes were brought together in William Caxton's *Mirrour of the World* (1480). Earthquakes are here again related to movements of subterranean fluids. Streams of water within Earth compress the air in hidden caverns. If the roofs of the caverns are weak, they rupture, causing cities and castles to fall into the chasms; if strong, they merely tremble and shake from the heaving by the wind below. Volcanic action follows if the outburst of wind and water from the depths is accompanied by fire and brimstone from hell.

The Chinese have the distinction of keeping the most faithful records of earthquakes and of inventing the first instrument capable of detecting them. Records of the dates on which major quakes rocked China date to 780 BCE. To detect quakes at a distance, the mathematician, astronomer, and geographer Zhang Heng (78–139 CE) invented what has been called the first seismograph.

KNOWLEDGE OF EARTH HISTORY

The occurrence of seashells embedded in the hard rocks of high mountains aroused the curiosity of early naturalists and eventually set off a controversy on the origin of fossils that continued through the 17th century. Xenophanes of Colophon (flourished *c.* 560 BCE) was credited by later writers with observing that seashells occur "in the midst of earth and in mountains." He is said to have believed that these relics originated during a catastrophic event that caused earth to be mixed with the sea and then to settle, burying organisms in the drying mud. For these

Fossilized leaf. PhotoObjects.net/Jupiterimages

views Xenophanes is sometimes called the father of paleontology.

Petrified wood was described by Chinese scholars as early as the 9th century CE and, about 1080, Shen Gua cited fossilized plants as evidence for change in climate. Other kinds of fossils that attracted the attention of early Chinese writers include spiriferoid brachiopods ("stone swallows"), cephalopods, crabs, and the bones and teeth of reptiles, birds, and mammals. Although these objects were commonly collected simply as curiosities or for medicinal

FOSSILS

A fossil is a remnant, impression, or trace of an animal or plant of a past geologic age that has been preserved in Earth's crust. The complex of data recorded in fossils worldwide—known as the fossil record—is the primary source of information about the history of life on Earth.

Fossilized footprint of an unidentified dinosaur. © Getty Images

Only a small fraction of ancient organisms are preserved as fossils. Usually only organisms that have a solid and resistant skeleton (vertebrates) are readily preserved. Most major groups of invertebrate animals have a calcareous skeleton or shell (e.g., corals, mollusks, brachiopods). Other forms have shells of calcium phosphate (which also occurs in the bones of vertebrates) or silicon dioxide. A shell or bone that is buried quickly after deposition may retain these organic tissues, though they become petrified (converted to a stony substance) over time. Unaltered hard parts, such as the shells of clams or brachiopods, are relatively common in sedimentary rocks, and some are quite old.

The hard parts of organisms that become buried in sediment may be subject to a variety of other changes during their conversion to solid rock, however. Solutions may fill the interstices, or pores, of the shell or bone with calcium carbonate or other mineral salts and thus fossilize the remains, in a process known as permineralization.

In other cases there may be a total replacement of the original skeletal material by other mineral matter, a process known as mineralization, or replacement. In still other cases, circulating acid solutions may dissolve the original shell but leave a cavity corresponding to it, and circulating solutions of calcium carbonate or silica may then deposit a new matrix in the cavity, thus creating a new impression of the original shell.

By contrast, the soft parts of animals or plants are very rarely preserved. The embedding of insects in amber and the preservation of the carcasses of Pleistocene-era mammoths in ice are rare but striking examples of the fossil preservation of soft tissues. Traces of organisms may also occur as tracks or trails or even borings.

The study of the fossil record has provided important information for at least four different purposes. The progressive changes observed within an animal group are used to describe the evolution of that group. Fossils also provide the geologist a quick and easy way of assigning a relative age to the strata in which they occur. The precision with which this may be done in any particular case depends on the nature and abundance of the animal, since some fossil groups were deposited during much longer time intervals than others. Fossils used to identify geologic relationships are known as index fossils.

purposes, Shen Gua recognized marine invertebrate fossils for what they are and for what they imply historically. Observing seashells in strata of the Taihang Mountains, he concluded that this region, though now far from the sea, must once have been a shore.

KNOWLEDGE OF LANDFORMS AND OF LAND-SEA RELATIONS

Changes in the landscape and in the position of land and sea related to erosion and deposition by streams were recognized by some early writers. The Greek historian Herodotus (c. 484–c. 426 BCE) correctly concluded that the northward bulge of Egypt into the Mediterranean is caused by the deposition of mud carried by the Nile.

The early Chinese writers were not outdone by the Romans and Greeks in their appreciation of changes wrought by erosion. In the *Jinshu* ("History of the Jin Dynasty"), it is said of Du Yu (222–284 CE) that when he ordered monumental stelae to be carved with the records of his successes, he had one buried at the foot of a mountain and the other erected on top. He predicted that in time they would likely change their relative positions, because the high hills will become valleys and the deep valleys will become hills.

Aristotle guessed that changes in the position of land and sea might be cyclical in character, thus reflecting some sort of natural order. If the rivers of a moist region should build deltas at their mouths, he reasoned, seawater would be displaced and the level of the sea would rise to cover some adjacent dry region. A reversal of climatic conditions might cause the sea to return to the area from which it had previously been displaced and retreat from the area previously inundated. The idea of a cyclical interchange between land and sea was elaborated in the *Discourses of the Brothers of Purity*, a classic Arabic work written between 941 and 982 CE by an anonymous group of scholars at Basra (Iraq). The rocks of the lands disintegrate and rivers carry their wastage to the sea, where waves and currents spread it over the seafloor. There the layers of sediment accumulate one above the other, harden, and, in the course of time, rise from the bottom of the sea to form new continents. Then the process of disintegration and leveling begins again.

THE 16TH–18TH CENTURIES

After the inspired beginnings of the ancient Greeks, Romans, Chinese, and Arabs, little or no new information was collected, and no new ideas were produced throughout the Middle Ages, much of which was appropriately called the Dark Ages. It was not until the Renaissance in the early 16th century that the geological sciences began to develop again.

Ore Deposits and Mineralogy

A common belief among alchemists of the 16th and 17th centuries held that metalliferous deposits were generated by heat emanating from Earth's centre but activated by the heavenly bodies.

The German scientist Georgius Agricola has with much justification been called the father of mineralogy. Of his seven geologic books, *De natura fossilium* (1546; "On Natural Fossils") contains his major contributions to mineralogy and, in fact, has been called the first textbook on that subject. In Agricola's time and well into the 19th century, "fossil" was a term that could be applied to any object dug from the Earth. Thus Agricola's classification of fossils provided pigeonholes for organic remains, such as ammonites, and for rocks of various kinds in addition to minerals. Individual kinds of minerals, their associations and manners of occurrence, are described in detail, many for the first time.

With the birth of analytical chemistry toward the latter part of the 18th century, the classification of minerals on the basis of their composition at last became possible. The German geologist Abraham Gottlob Werner was one of those who favoured a chemical classification in preference to a "natural history" classification based on external appearances. His list of several classifications, published posthumously, recognized 317 different substances ordered in four classes.

PALEONTOLOGY AND STRATIGRAPHY

During the 17th century the guiding principles of paleontology and historical geology began to emerge in the work of a few individuals. Nicolaus Steno, a Danish scientist and theologian, presented carefully reasoned arguments favouring the organic origin of what are now called fossils. Also, he elucidated three principles that made possible the reconstruction of certain kinds of geologic events in a chronological order. In his *Canis carcariae dissectum caput* (1667; "Dissected Head of a Dog Shark"), he concluded that large tongue-shaped objects found in the strata of Malta were the teeth of sharks, whose remains were buried beneath the seafloor and later raised out of the water to their present sites.

This excursion into paleontology led Steno to confront a broader question. How can one solid body, such as a shark's tooth, become embedded in another solid body, such as a layer of rock? He published his answers in 1669 in a paper titled "De solido intra naturaliter contento dissertationis" ("A Preliminary Discourse Concerning a Solid Body Enclosed by Processes of Nature Within a Solid"). Steno cited evidence to show that when the hard parts of an organism are covered with sediment, it is they and not the aggregates of sediment that are firm. Consolidation of the sediment into rock may come later, and, if so, the original solid fossil becomes encased in solid rock. He recognized that sediments settle from fluids layer by layer to form strata that are originally continuous and nearly horizontal. His principle of superposition of strata states that in a sequence of strata, as originally laid down, any stratum is younger than the one on which it rests and older than the one that rests upon it.

In 1667 and 1668 the English physicist Robert Hooke read papers before the Royal Society in which he expressed many of the ideas contained in Steno's works. Hooke argued for the organic nature of fossils. Elevation of beds containing marine fossils to mountainous heights he attributed to the work of earthquakes. Streams attacking these elevated tracts wear down the hills, fill depressions with sediment, and thus level out irregularities of the landscape.

EARTH HISTORY ACCORDING TO WERNER AND JAMES HUTTON

The two major theories of the 18th century were the Neptunian and the Plutonian. The Neptunists, led by Abraham Gottlob Werner and his students, maintained that Earth was originally covered by a turbid ocean. The first sediments deposited over the irregular floor of this universal ocean formed the granite and other crystalline rocks. Then as the ocean began to subside, "stratified" rocks were laid down in succession. The "volcanic" rocks were the youngest; Neptunists took small account of volcanism and thought that lava was formed by the burning of coal deposits underground.

The Scottish scientist James Hutton, leader of the Plutonists, viewed Earth as a dynamic body that functions as a heat machine. Streams wear down the continents and deposit their waste in the sea. Subterranean heat causes the outer part of Earth to expand in places, uplifting the compacted marine sediments to form new continents. Hutton recognized that granite is an intrusive igneous rock and not a primitive sediment as the Neptunists claimed. Intrusive sills and dikes of igneous rock provide evidence for the driving force of subterranean heat. Hutton viewed great angular unconformities separating sedimentary sequences as evidence for past cycles of sedimentation, uplift, and erosion. His *Theory of the Earth*, published as an essay in 1788, was expanded to a two-volume work in 1795. John Playfair, a professor of natural philosophy, defended Hutton against the counterattacks of the Neptunists, and his *Illustrations of the Huttonian Theory* (1802) is the clearest contemporary account of Plutonist theory.

CATASTROPHISM AND UNIFORMITARIANISM

Catastrophism is the doctrine that explains the differences in fossil forms encountered in successive stratigraphic levels as being the product of repeated cataclysmic occurrences and repeated new creations. This doctrine generally is associated with the great French naturalist Baron Georges Cuvier (1769–1832). One 20th-century expansion on Cuvier's views, in effect, a neocatastrophic school, attempts to explain geologic history as a sequence of rhythms or pulsations of mountain building, transgression and regression of the seas, and evolution and extinction of living organisms.

Uniformitarianism, however, differs significantly from catastrophism. Uniformitarianism is the doctrine that existing processes acting in the same manner and with essentially the same intensity as at present are sufficient to account for all geologic change. It posits that natural agents now at work on and within Earth have operated with general uniformity through immensely long periods of time. When William Whewell, a University of Cambridge scholar, introduced the term in 1832, the prevailing view (called catastrophism) was that Earth had originated through supernatural means and had been affected by a series of catastrophic events such as the biblical Flood. In contrast to the catastrophic view of geology, the principle of uniformity postulates that phenomena displayed in the rocks may be entirely accounted for by geologic processes that continue to operate present day—in other words, the present is the key to the past. This principle is fundamental to geologic thinking and underlies the whole development of the science of geology. The term *uniformitarianism*, however, has passed into history, for the controversy between catastrophists and uniformitarians has largely died. Geology as an applied science draws on the other sciences, but in the early 19th century geologic discovery had outrun the physics and chemistry of the day. As geologic phenomena became explicable in terms of advancing physics, chemistry, and biology, the reality of the principle of uniformity as a major philosophical tenet of geology became established and the controversy ended.

THE 19TH CENTURY

The 19th century was a period of rapid development in the geologic sciences. The first forays into crystallography were made during this time. In addition, the 19th century saw the rise of uniformitarianism, the development of the principal of faunal succession, and attempts to describe geologic time.

CRYSTALLOGRAPHY AND THE CLASSIFICATION OF MINERALS AND ROCKS

The French scientist René-Just Häuy, whose treatises on mineralogy and crystallography appeared in 1801 and 1822, respectively, has been credited with advancing mineralogy to the status of a science and with establishing the science of crystallography. From his studies of the geometric relationships between planes of cleavage, he concluded that the ultimate particles forming a given species of mineral have the same shape and that variations in crystal habit reflect differences in the ways identical molecules are put together. In 1814 Jöns Jacob Berzelius of Sweden published a system of mineralogy offering a comprehensive classification of minerals based on their chemistry. Berzelius recognized silica as an acid and introduced into mineralogy the group known as silicates. At mid-century the American geologist James Dwight Dana's *System of Mineralogy*, in its third edition, was reorganized around a chemical classification, which thereafter became standard for handbooks.

The development of the polarizing microscope and the technique for grinding sections of rocks so thin as to be virtually transparent came in 1827 from studies of fossilized wood by William Nicol. In 1849 Clifton Sorby showed that minerals viewed in thin section could be identified by their optical properties, and soon afterward improved classifications of rocks were made on the basis of their mineralogic composition. The German geologist Ferdinand Zirkel's *Mikroscopische Beschaffenheit der Mineralien und Gesteine* (1873; "The Microscopic Nature of Minerals and Rocks") contains one of the first mineralogic classifications of rocks and marks the emergence of microscopic petrography as an established branch of science.

WILLIAM SMITH AND FAUNAL SUCCESSION

In 1683 the zoologist Martin Lister proposed to the Royal Society that a new sort of map be drawn showing the areal distribution of the different kinds of British "soiles" (vegetable soils and underlying bedrock). The work proposed by Lister was not accomplished until 132 years later, when William Smith published his *Geologic Map of England and Wales with Part of Scotland* (1815).

A self-educated surveyor and engineer, Smith had the habit of collecting fossils and making careful note of the strata that contained them. He discovered that the different stratified formations in England contain distinctive assemblages of fossils. His map, reproduced on a scale of five miles to the inch, showed 20 different rock units, to which Smith applied local names in common use—e.g., London Clay and Purbeck Beds. In 1816 Smith published a companion work, *Strata Identified by Organized Fossils*, in which the organic remains characteristic of each of his rock units were illustrated. His generalization that each formation is "possessed of properties peculiar to itself [and] has the same organized fossils throughout its course" is the first clear statement of the principle of faunal sequence, which is the basis for worldwide correlation of fossiliferous strata into a coherent system. Smith thus demonstrated two kinds of order in nature: order in the spatial arrangement of rock units and order in the succession of ancient forms of life.

Smith's principle of faunal sequence was another way of saying that there are discontinuities in the sequences of fossilized plants and animals. These discontinuities were interpreted as indicators of episodic destruction of life or as evidence for the incompleteness of the fossil record. Baron Georges Cuvier of France was one of the more distinguished members of a large group of naturalists who believed that paleontological discontinuities bore witness to sudden and widespread catastrophes. Cuvier's skill at comparative anatomy enabled him to reconstruct from fragmentary remains the skeletons of large vertebrate animals found at different levels in the Cenozoic sequence of northern France. From these studies he discovered that the fossils in all but the youngest deposits belong to species now extinct. Moreover, these extinct species have definite ranges up and down in the stratigraphic column. Cuvier inferred that the successive extinctions were the result of convulsions that caused the strata of the continents to be dislocated and folded and the seas to sweep across the continents and just as suddenly subside.

CHARLES LYELL AND UNIFORMITARIANISM

In opposition to the catastrophist school of thought, the British geologist Charles Lyell proposed a uniformitarian interpretation of geologic history in his *Principles of Geology* (3 vol., 1830–33). His system was based on two propositions: the causes of geologic change operating include all the causes that have acted from the earliest time; and these causes have always operated at the same average levels of energy. These two propositions add up to a "steady-state" theory of Earth. Changes in climate have fluctuated around a mean, reflecting changes in the position of land and sea. Progress through time in the organic world is likewise an illusion, the effect of an imperfect paleontological record.

The main part of the *Principles* was devoted less to theory than to procedures for inferring events from rocks. For Lyell's clear exposition of methodology, his work was highly regarded throughout its many editions, long after the author himself had abandoned antiprogressivist views on the development of life.

Charles Lyell. Hulton Archive/Getty Images

LOUIS AGASSIZ AND THE ICE AGE

Huge boulders of granite resting upon limestone of the Jura Mountains were subjects of controversy during the 18th and early 19th centuries. Saussure described these in 1779 and called them erratics. He concluded that they had been swept to their present positions by torrents of water. Saussure's interpretation was in accord with the tenets of diluvial geologists, who interpreted erratics and sheets of unstratified sediment (till or drift) spread over the northern parts of Europe and North America as the work of the "Deluge."

In 1837 the Swiss zoologist and paleontologist Louis Agassiz delivered a startling address before the Helvetian Society, proposing that, during a geologically recent stage of refrigeration, glacial ice had covered Eurasia from the North Pole to the shores of the Mediterranean and Caspian seas. Wherever erratics, till, and striated pavements of rock occur, sure evidence of this recent catastrophe exists. The reception accorded this address was glacial, too, and Alexander von Humboldt advised Agassiz to return to

ERRATICS

Glacier-transported rock fragments that differ from the local bedrock are called erratics. Erratics may be embedded in till or occur on the ground surface and may range in size from pebbles to huge boulders weighing thousands of tons. The distance of transportation may range from less than 1 km (0.6 mile) to more than 800 km (500 miles); those transported over long distances generally consist of rock resistant to the shattering and grinding effects of glacial transport. Erratics composed of unusual and distinctive rock types can be traced to their source of origin and serve as indicators of the direction of glacial movement. Studies making use of such indicator erratics have provided information on the general origins and flow paths of the major ice sheets and on the locations of important mineral deposits. Erratics played an important part in the initial recognition of the last ice age and its extent. Originally thought to be transported by gigantic floods or by ice rafting, erratics were first explained in terms of glacial transport by the Swiss-American naturalist and geologist J.L.R. Agassiz in 1840.

his fossil fishes. Instead, he began intensive field studies and in 1840 published his *Études sur les glaciers* ("Studies of Glaciers"), demonstrating that Alpine glaciers had been far more extensive in the past. That same year he visited the British Isles in the company of Buckland and extended the glacial doctrine to Scotland, northern England, and Ireland. In 1846 he carried his campaign to North America and there found additional evidence for an ice age.

GEOLOGIC TIME AND THE AGE OF EARTH

By mid-century the fossiliferous strata of Europe had been grouped into systems arrayed in chronological order. The stratigraphic column, a composite of these systems, was pieced together from exposures in different regions by application of the principles of superposition and faunal sequence. Time elapsed during the formation of a system became known as a period, and the periods were grouped into eras: the Paleozoic (Cambrian through Permian periods), Mesozoic (Triassic, Jurassic, and Cretaceous periods), and Cenozoic (Paleogene, Neogene, and Quaternary periods).

Charles Darwin's *Origin of Species* (1859) offered a theoretical explanation for the empirical principle of faunal sequence. The fossils of the successive systems are different not only because parts of the stratigraphic record are missing but also because most species have lost in their struggles for survival and also because those that do survive evolve into new forms over time. Darwin borrowed two ideas from Lyell and the uniformitarians: that geologic time is virtually without limit and that a sequence of minute changes integrated over long periods of time produce remarkable changes in natural entities.

The evolutionists and the historical geologists were embarrassed when, beginning in 1864, William Thomson (later Baron Kelvin) attacked the steady-state theory

William Thomson, Baron Kelvin, 1869.
© Photos.com/Thinkstock

of Earth and placed numerical strictures on the length of geologic time. Earth might function as a heat machine, but it could not also be a perpetual motion machine. Assuming that Earth was originally molten, Thomson calculated that not less than 20 million and not more than 400 million years could have passed since Earth first became a solid body. Other physicists of note put even narrower limits on Earth's age ranging down to 15 million or 20 million years. All these calculations, however, were based on the common assumption, not always explicitly stated, that Earth's substance is inert and hence incapable of generating new heat. Shortly before the end of the century this assumption was negated by the discovery of radioactive elements that disintegrate spontaneously and release heat to Earth in the process.

CONCEPTS OF LANDFORM EVOLUTION

The scientific exploration of the American West following the end of the Civil War yielded much new information on the sculpture of the landscape by streams. In his reports on the Colorado River and Uinta Mountains (1875, 1876), John Wesley Powell explained how streams may come to flow across mountain ranges rather than detour around them. The Green River does not follow some structural crack in its gorge across the Uinta Mountains; instead it has cut its canyon as the mountain range was slowly bowed up. Given enough time, streams will erode their drainage basins to plains approaching sea level as a base.

Grove Karl Gilbert's *Report on the Geology of the Henry Mountains* (1877) offered a detailed analysis of fluvial processes. According to Gilbert, all streams work toward a graded condition, a state of dynamic equilibrium that is attained when the net effect of the flowing water is neither erosion of the bed nor deposition of sediment, when the landscape reflects a balance between the resistance of the rocks to erosion and the processes that are operative upon them.

After 1884 William Morris Davis developed the concept of the geographical cycle, during which elevated regions pass through successive stages of dissection and denudation characterized as youthful, mature, and old. Youthful landscapes have broad divides and narrow valleys. With further denudation the original surface on which the streams began their work is reduced to ridgetops. Finally in the stage of old age, the region is reduced to a nearly featureless plain near sea level or its inland projection. Uplift of the region in any stage of this evolution will activate a new cycle. Davis's views dominated geomorphic thought until well into the 20th century, when quantitative approaches resulted in the rediscovery of Gilbert's ideas.

Gravity, Isostasy, and Earth's Figure

Discoveries of regional anomalies in Earth's gravity led to the realization that high mountain ranges have underlying deficiencies in mass about equal to the apparent surface loads represented by the mountains themselves. In the 18th century the French scientist Pierre Bouguer had observed that the deflections of the pendulum in Peru are much less than they should be if the

Andes represent a load perched on top of Earth's crust. Similar anomalies were later found to obtain along the Himalayan front. To explain these anomalies it was necessary to assume that beneath some depth within Earth pressures are hydrostatic (equal on all sides). If excess loads are placed upon the crust, as by addition of a continental ice cap, the crust will sink to compensate for the additional mass and will rise again when the load is removed. The tendency toward general equilibrium maintained through vertical movements of Earth's outer layers was called isostasy in 1899 by Clarence Edward Dutton of the United States.

Evidence for substantial vertical movements of the crust was supplied by studies of regional stratigraphy. In 1883 another American geologist, James Hall, had demonstrated that Paleozoic rocks of the folded Appalachians were several times as thick as sequences of the same age in the plateaus and plains to the west. It was his conclusion that the folded strata in the mountains must have accumulated in a linear submarine trough that filled with sediment as it subsided. Downward crustal flexures of this magnitude came to be called geosynclines.

THE 20TH CENTURY

The development of the geologic sciences in the 20th century has been influenced by two major "revolutions." The first involves dramatic technological advances that have resulted in vastly improved instrumentation, the prime examples being the many types of highly sophisticated computerized devices. The second is centred on the development of the plate tectonics theory, which is the most profound and influential conceptual advance the Earth sciences have ever known.

ISOSTASY

Isostasy is the ideal theoretical balance of all large portions of Earth's lithosphere as though they were floating on the denser underlying layer, the asthenosphere. The asthenosphere is a section of the upper mantle composed of weak, plastic rock that is about 110 km (70 miles) below the surface. Isostasy controls the regional elevations of continents and ocean floors in accordance with the densities of their underlying rocks. Imaginary columns of equal cross-sectional area that rise from the asthenosphere to the surface are assumed to have equal weights everywhere on Earth, even though their constituents and the elevations of their upper surfaces are significantly different. This means that an excess of mass seen as material above sea level, as in a mountain system, is due to a deficit of mass, or low-density roots, below sea level. Therefore, high mountains have low-density roots that extend deep into the underlying mantle. The concept of isostasy played an important role in the development of the theory of plate tectonics.

In 1735, expeditions over the Andes led by Pierre Bouguer, a French photometrist and the first to measure the horizontal gravitational pull of mountains, noted that the Andes could not represent a protuberance of rock sitting on a solid platform. If it did, then a plumb-line should be deflected from the true vertical by an amount proportional to the gravitational attraction of the mountain range. The deflection was less than that which was anticipated. About a century later, similar discrepancies were observed by Sir George Everest, surveyor general of India, in surveys south of the Himalayas, indicating a lack of compensating mass beneath the visible mountain ranges.

In the theory of isostasy, a mass above sea level is supported below sea level, and there is thus a certain depth at which the total weight per unit area is equal all around Earth; this is known as the depth of compensation. The depth of compensation was taken to be 113 km (70 miles) according to the Hayford-Bowie concept, named for American geodesists John Fillmore Hayford and William Bowie. Owing to changing tectonic environments, however, perfect isostasy is approached but rarely attained, and some regions, such as oceanic trenches and high plateaus, are not isostatically compensated.

Modern technological developments have affected all the different geologic disciplines. Their impact has been particularly notable in such activities as radiometric dating, experimental petrology, crystallography, chemical analysis of rocks and minerals, micropaleontology, and seismological exploration of Earth's deep interior.

RADIOMETRIC DATING

In 1905, shortly after the discovery of radioactivity, the American chemist Bertram Boltwood suggested that lead is one of the disintegration products of uranium, in which case the older a uranium-bearing mineral the greater should be its proportional part of lead. Analyzing specimens whose relative geologic ages were known, Boltwood found that the ratio of lead to uranium did indeed increase with age. After estimating the rate of this radioactive change, he calculated that the absolute ages of his specimens ranged from 410 million to 2.2 billion years. Though his figures were too high by about 20 percent, their order of magnitude was enough to dispose of the short scale of geologic time proposed by Lord Kelvin.

Versions of the modern mass spectrometer were invented in the early 1920s and 1930s, and during World War II the device was improved substantially to help in the development of the atomic bomb. Soon after the war, Harold C. Urey and G.J. Wasserburg applied the mass spectrometer to the study of geochronology. This device separates the different isotopes of the same element and can measure the variations in these isotopic abundances to within one part in 10,000. By determining the amount of the parent and daughter isotopes present in a sample and by knowing their rate of radioactive decay (eachradioisotope has its own decay constant), the isotopic age of the sample can be calculated. For dating minerals and

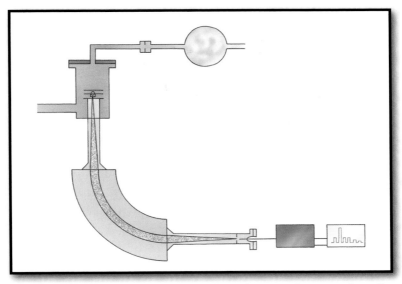

Illustration of a mass spectrometer, used by geologists to determine the radioactive age of a rock sample. Dorling Kindersley/Getty Images

rocks, investigators commonly use the following couplets of parent and daughter isotopes: thorium-232–lead-208, uranium-235–lead-207, samarium-147–neodymium-143, rubidium-87–strontium-87, potassium-40–argon-40, and argon-40–argon-39.

The SHRIMP (Sensitive High Resolution Ion Microprobe) enables the accurate determination of the uranium-lead age of the mineral zircon, and this has revolutionized the understanding of the isotopic age of formation of zircon-bearing igneous granitic rocks. Another technological development is the ICP-MS (Inductively Coupled Plasma Mass Spectrometer), which is able to provide the isotopic age of the minerals zircon, titanite, rutile, and monazite. These minerals are common to many igneous and metamorphic rocks.

Such techniques have had an enormous impact on scientific knowledge of Earth history because precise dates can now be obtained on rocks in all orogenic (mountain) belts ranging in age from the early Archean (about 4 billion years old) to the early Neogene (roughly 20 million years old). The oldest known rocks on Earth, estimated at 4.28 billion years old, are the faux amphibolite volcanic deposits of the Nuvvuagittuq greenstone belt in Quebec, Can. A radiometric dating technique that measures the ratio of the rare earth elements neodymium and samarium present in a rock sample was used to produce the estimate. Also, by extrapolating backward in time to a situation when there was no lead that had been produced by radiogenic processes, a figure of about 4.6 billion years is obtained for the minimum age of Earth. This figure is of the same order as ages obtained for certain meteorites and lunar rocks.

EXPERIMENTAL STUDY OF ROCKS

Experimental petrology began with the work of Jacobus Henricus van 't Hoff, one of the founders of physical chemistry. Between 1896 and 1908 he elucidated the complex sequence of chemical reactions attending the precipitation of salts (evaporites) from the evaporation of seawater. Van 't Hoff's aim was to explain the succession of mineral salts present in Permian rocks of Germany. His success at producing from aqueous solutions artificial minerals and rocks like those found in natural salt deposits stimulated studies of minerals crystallizing from silicate melts simulating the magmas from which igneous rocks have formed. Working at the Geophysical Laboratory of the Carnegie Institution of Washington, D.C., Norman L. Bowen conducted extensive phase-equilibrium studies of silicate systems, brought together in his *Evolution of the Igneous Rocks* (1928). Experimental petrology, both at the low-temperature range explored by van 't Hoff and in the high ranges of temperature investigated by Bowen, continues to provide laboratory evidence for interpreting the chemical history of sedimentary and igneous rocks. Experimental petrology also provides valuable data on the stability limits of individual metamorphic minerals and of the reactions between different minerals in a wide variety of chemical systems. These experiments are carried out at elevated temperatures and pressures that simulate those operating in different levels of Earth's crust. Thus the metamorphic petrologist today can compare the minerals and mineral assemblages found in natural rocks with comparable examples produced in the laboratory, the pressure–temperature limits of which have been well defined by experimental petrology.

Another branch of experimental science relates to the deformation of rocks. In 1906 the American physicist P. W. Bridgman developed a technique for subjecting rock samples to high pressures similar to those deep within Earth. Studies of the behaviour of rocks in the laboratory have shown that their strength increases with confining pressure but decreases with rise in temperature. Down to depths of a few kilometres the strength of rocks would be expected to increase. At greater depths the temperature effect should become dominant, and response to stress should result in flow rather than fracture of rocks. In 1959 two American geologists, Marion King Hubbertand William W. Rubey, demonstrated that fluids in the pores of rock may reduce internal friction and permit gliding over nearly horizontal planes of the large overthrust blocks associated with folded mountains. More recently the Norwegian petrologist Hans Ramberg performed many experiments with a large centrifuge that produced a negative gravity effect and thus was able to create structures simulating salt domes, which rise because of the relatively low density of the salt in comparison with that of surrounding rocks. With all these deformation experiments, it is necessary to scale down as precisely as possible variables such as the time and velocity of the experiment and the viscosity and temperature of the material from the natural to the laboratory conditions.

CRYSTALLOGRAPHY

In the 19th century crystallographers were able to study only the external form of minerals. It was not until 1895, when the German physicist Wilhelm Conrad Röntgen discovered X-rays, that it became possible to consider their internal structure. In 1912 another German physicist, Max von Laue, realized that X-rays were scattered and deflected at regular angles when they passed through a copper sulfate crystal, and so he produced the first X-ray diffraction pattern on a photographic film.

A year later William Bragg of Britain and his son Lawrence perceived that such a pattern reflects the layers of atoms in the crystal structure, and they succeeded in determining for the first time the atomic crystal structure of the mineral halite (sodium chloride). These discoveries had a long-lasting influence on crystallography because they led to the development of the X-ray powder diffractometer, which is now widely used to identify minerals and to ascertain their crystal structure.

THE CHEMICAL ANALYSIS OF
ROCKS AND MINERALS

Advanced analytic chemical equipment has revolutionized the understanding of the composition of rocks and minerals. For example, the XRF (X-Ray Fluorescence) spectrometer can quantify the major and trace element abundances of many chemical elements in a rock sample down to parts-per-million concentrations. This geochemical method has been used to differentiate successive stages of igneous rocks in the plate-tectonic cycle. The metamorphic petrologist can use the bulk composition of a recrystallized rock to define the structure of the original rock, assuming that no structural change has occurred during the metamorphic process. Next, the electron microprobe bombards a thin microscopic slice of a mineral in a sample with a beam of electrons, which can determine the chemical composition of the mineral almost instantly. This method has wide applications in, for example, the fields of industrial mineralogy, materials science, igneous geochemistry, and metamorphic petrology.

MICROPALEONTOLOGY

Microscopic fossils, such as ostracods, foraminifera, and pollen grains, are common in sediments of the Mesozoic and Cenozoic eras (from about 251 million years ago to the present). Because the rock chips brought up in oil wells are so small, a high-resolution instrument known as a scanning electron microscope had to be developed to study the microfossils. The classification of microfossils of organisms that lived within relatively short time spans has enabled Mesozoic-Cenozoic sediments to be subdivided in remarkable detail. This technique also has had a major impact on the study of Precambrian life (i.e., organisms that existed more than 542 million years ago). Carbonaceous spheroids and filaments about 7–10 mm (0.3–0.4 inch) long are recorded in 3.5 billion-year-old sediments in the Pilbara region of northwestern Western

Australia and in the lower Onverwacht Series of the Barberton belt in South Africa; these are the oldest reliable records of life on Earth.

SEISMOLOGY AND THE STRUCTURE OF EARTH

Earthquake study was institutionalized in 1880 with the formation of the Seismological Society of Japan under the leadership of the English geologist John Milne. He and his associates invented the first accurate seismographs, including the instrument later known as the Milne seismograph. Seismology has revealed much about the structure of Earth's core, mantle, and crust. The English seismologist Richard Dixon Oldham's studies of earthquake records in 1906 led to the discovery of Earth's core. From studies of the Croatian quake of Oct. 8, 1909, the geophysicist Andrija Mohorovičić discovered the discontinuity (often called the Moho) that separates the crust from the underlying mantle.

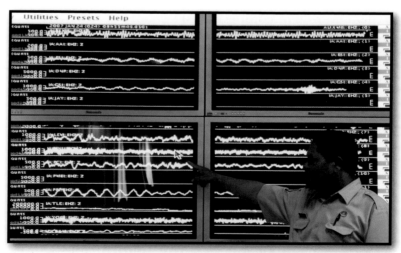

At the Bengkulu (Indonesia) Meteorology and Geophysics Agency offices, a geophysicist points to a spot on a projected seismograph reading that indicates when an earthquake struck the area in 2007. Dimas Ardian/Getty Images

Today there are more than 1,000 seismograph stations around the world, and their data are used to compile seismicity maps. These maps show that earthquake epicentres are aligned in narrow, continuous belts along the boundaries of lithospheric plates. The earthquake foci outline the mid-oceanic ridges in the Atlantic, Pacific, and Indian oceans where the plates separate, while around the margins of the Pacific where the plates converge, they lie in a dipping plane, or Benioff zone, that defines the position of the subducting plate boundary to depths of about 700 km (435 miles).

Since 1950, additional information on the crust has been obtained from the analysis of artificial tremors produced by chemical explosions. These studies have shown that the Moho is present under all continents at an average depth of 35 km (22 miles) and that the crust above it thickens under young mountain ranges to depths of 70 km (about 44 miles) in the Andes and the Himalayas. In such investigations the reflections of the seismic waves generated from a series of "shot" points are also recorded, and this makes it possible to construct a profile of the subsurface structure. This is seismic reflection profiling, the main method of exploration used by the petroleum industry. During the late 1970s a new technique for generating seismic waves was invented: thumping and vibrating the surface of the ground with a gas-propelled piston from a large truck.

The Theory of Plate Tectonics

Plate tectonics has revolutionized virtually every discipline of the Earth sciences since the late 1960s and early 1970s. It has served as a unifying model or paradigm for explaining geologic phenomena that were formerly considered in unrelated fashion. Plate tectonics describes

SEISMOLOGY

Seismology is the scientific discipline that is concerned with the study of earthquakes and of the propagation of seismic waves within Earth. A branch of geophysics, it has provided much information about the composition and state of the planet's interior.

The goals of seismological investigations may be local or regional, as in the attempt to determine subsurface faults and other structures in petroleum or mineral exploration, or they may be of global significance, as in attempts to determine structural discontinuities in Earth's interior, the geophysical characteristics of island arcs, oceanic trenches, or mid-oceanic ridges, or the elastic properties of Earth materials generally.

In recent years, attention has been devoted to earthquake prediction and, more successfully, to assessing seismic hazards at different geographic sites in an effort to reduce the risks of earthquakes. The physics of seismic fault sources have been better determined and modeled for computer analysis. Moreover, seismologists have studied quakes induced by human activities, such as impounding water behind high dams and detonating underground nuclear explosions. The objective of the latter research is to find ways of discriminating between explosions and natural earthquakes.

seismic activity, volcanism, mountain building, and various other Earth processes in terms of the structure and mechanical behaviour of a small number of enormous rigid plates thought to constitute the outer part of the planet (i.e., the lithosphere). This all-encompassing theory grew out of observations and ideas about continental drift and seafloor spreading.

In 1912 the German meteorologist Alfred Wegener proposed that throughout most of geologic time there was only one continental mass, which he named Pangea. At some time during the Mesozoic Era, Pangaea fragmented and the parts began to drift apart. Westward drift of the

Americas opened the Atlantic Ocean, and the Indian block drifted across the Equator to join with Asia. In 1937 the South African Alexander Du Toit modified Wegener's hypothesis by suggesting the existence of two primordial continents: Laurasia in the north and Gondwanaland in the south. Aside from the congruency of continental shelf margins across the Atlantic, proponents of continental drift have amassed impressive geologic evidence to support their views. Similarities in fossil terrestrial organisms in pre-Cretaceous (older than about 146 million years) strata of Africa and South America and in pre-Jurassic rocks (older than about 200 million years) of Australia, India, Madagascar, and Africa are explained if these continents were formerly connected but difficult to account for otherwise. Fitting the Americas with the continents across the Atlantic brings together similar kinds of rocks and structures. Evidence of widespread glaciation during the late Paleozoic is found in Antarctica, southern South America, southern Africa, India, and Australia. If these continents were formerly united around the South Polar region, this glaciation becomes explicable as a unified sequence of events in time and space.

Interest in continental drift heightened during the 1950s as knowledge of Earth's magnetic field during the geologic past developed from the studies of Stanley K. Runcorn, Patrick M.S. Blackett, and others. Ferromagnetic minerals such as magnetite acquire a permanent magnetization when they crystallize as components of igneous rock. The direction of their magnetization is the same as the direction of Earth's magnetic field at the place and time of crystallization. Particles of magnetized minerals released from their parent igneous rocks by weathering may later realign themselves with the existing magnetic field at the time these particles are incorporated into sedimentary deposits. Studies of the remanent magnetism in suitable rocks of different ages from over the world indicate that the magnetic poles were in different places at different times. The polar wandering curves are different for the several continents, but in important instances these differences are reconciled on the assumption that continents now separated were formerly joined. The curves for Europe and North America, for example, are reconciled by the assumption that America has drifted about 30° westward relative to Europe since the Triassic Period (approximately 251 million to 200 million years ago).

In the early 1960s a major breakthrough in understanding the way the modern Earth works came from two studies of the ocean floor. First, the American geophysicists Harry H. Hess and Robert S. Dietz suggested that new ocean crust was formed along mid-oceanic ridges between separating continents; and second, Drummond H. Matthews and Frederick J. Vine of Britain proposed that the new oceanic crust acted like a magnetic tape recorder insofar as magnetic anomaly strips parallel to the ridge had been magnetized alternately in normal and reversed order, reflecting the changes in polarity of Earth's magnetic field. This theory of seafloor spreading then needed testing, and the opportunity arose from major advances in deepwater drilling technology. The Joint Oceanographic Institutions Deep Earth Sampling (JOIDES) project began in 1969, continued with the Deep Sea Drilling Project (DSDP), and, since 1976, with the International Phase of Ocean Drilling (IPOD) project. These projects have produced more than 500 boreholes in the floor of the world's oceans, and the results have been as outstanding as the plate-tectonic theory itself. They confirm that the oceanic crust is everywhere younger than about 200 million years and that the stratigraphic age determined by micropaleontology of the overlying oceanic sediments is close to the age of the oceanic crust calculated from the magnetic anomalies.

The plate-tectonic theory, which embraces both continental drift and seafloor spreading, was formulated in the mid-1960s by the Canadian geologist J. Tuzo Wilson, who described the network of mid-oceanic ridges, transform faults, and subduction zones as boundaries separating an evolving mosaic of enormous plates, and who proposed the idea of the opening and closing of oceans and eventual production of an orogenic belt by the collision of two continents.

Up to this point, no one had considered in any detail the implications of the plate-tectonic theory for the evolution of continental orogenic belts; most thought had been devoted to the oceans. In 1969 John Dewey of the University of Cambridge outlined an analysis of the

REMANENT MAGNETISM

Remanent magnetism, which is also called paleomagnetism (or palaeomagnetism), is the permanent magnetism in rocks resulting from the orientation of Earth's magnetic field at the time of rock formation in a past geological age. It is the source of information for the paleomagnetic studies of polar wandering and continental drift. Remanent magnetism can derive from several natural processes, generally termed natural remanent magnetism, the most important being thermo-remanent magnetism. This arises when magnetic minerals forming in igneous rocks cool through the Curie point and when the magnetic domains within the individual minerals align themselves with Earth's magnetic field, thus making a permanent record of its orientation.

A second mechanism operates when small grains of magnetic minerals settle into a sedimentary matrix, producing detrital remanent magnetism. It is hypothesized that the tiny grains orient themselves in the direction of Earth's magnetic field during deposition and before the final consolidation of the rock. The magnetism thus introduced appears to persist through later alteration and compaction of the rock, although the details of these processes have not been fully studied.

Rocks may acquire remanent magnetism in at least two other ways: (1) rocks made up of nonmagnetic minerals may be chemically altered to yield magnetic minerals, and these newly formed minerals will acquire remanent magnetism in the presence of Earth's magnetic field; and (2) igneous rocks already cooled may ultimately acquire remanent magnetism by a process called viscous magnetization. The difference between these several types of remanent magnetism can be determined, and the magnetic history of a particular rock can therefore be interpreted.

Caledonian-Appalachian orogenic belts in terms of a complete plate-tectonic cycle of events, and this provided a model for the interpretation of other pre-Mesozoic (Paleozoic and Precambrian) belts. Even the oldest volcano-sedimentary rocks on Earth, in the 3.8 billion-year-old Isua belt in West Greenland, have been shown by geologists from the Tokyo Institute of Technology to have formed in a plate-tectonic setting—i.e., in a trench or mouth of a subduction zone.

CHAPTER 2
GEOLOGY

Geology and its subdisciplines make up the fields of study concerned with the solid Earth. Included are sciences such as mineralogy, geodesy, and stratigraphy. An introduction to the geochemical and geophysical sciences logically begins with mineralogy because Earth's rocks are composed of minerals—inorganic elements or compounds that have a fixed chemical composition and are made up of regularly aligned rows of atoms. Today, one of the principal concerns of mineralogy is the chemical analysis of the some 3,000 known minerals that are the chief constituents of the three different rock types: sedimentary (formed by diagenesis of sediments deposited by surface processes), igneous (crystallized from magmas either at depth or at the surface as lavas), and metamorphic (formed by a recrystallization process at temperatures and pressures in Earth's crust high enough to destabilize the parent sedimentary or igneous material). Geochemistry is the study of the composition of these different types of rocks.

During mountain building, rocks became highly deformed, and the primary objective of structural geology is to elucidate the mechanism of formation of the many types of structures (e.g., folds and faults) that arise from such deformation. The allied field of geophysics has several subdisciplines, which make use of different instrumental techniques. Seismology, for example, involves the exploration of Earth's deep structure through the detailed analysis of recordings of elastic waves generated by earthquakes and man-made explosions. Earthquake seismology has largely been responsible for defining the location of major plate boundaries and of the dip of subduction zones down to depths of about 700 km (435 miles) at those boundaries. In other subdisciplines of geophysics, gravimetric techniques are used to determine the shape and size of underground structures, electrical methods help locate a variety of mineral deposits that tend to be good conductors of electricity, and paleomagnetism has played the principal role in tracking the drift of continents.

Geomorphology is concerned with the surface processes that create the landscapes of the world—namely, weathering and erosion. Weathering is the alteration and breakdown of rocks at Earth's surface caused by local atmospheric conditions, while erosion is the process by which the weathering products are removed by water, ice, and wind. The combination of weathering and erosion leads to the wearing down or denudation of mountains and continents, with the erosion products being deposited in rivers, internal drainage basins, and the oceans. Erosion is thus the complement of deposition. The unconsolidated accumulated sediments are transformed by the process of diagenesis and lithification into sedimentary rocks, thereby completing a full cycle of the transfer of matter from an old continent to a young ocean and ultimately to the formation of new sedimentary rocks.

Knowledge of the processes of interaction of the atmosphere and the hydrosphere with the surface rocks and soils of Earth's crust is important for an understanding not only of the development of landscapes, but also (and perhaps more importantly) the ways in which sediments are created. This, in turn, helps in interpreting the mode of formation and the depositional environment of sedimentary rocks. Thus the discipline of geomorphology is fundamental to the uniformitarian approach to the Earth sciences, according to which the present is the key to the past.

Geologic history provides a conceptual framework and overview of the evolution of Earth. An early development of the subject was stratigraphy, the study of order and sequence in bedded sedimentary rocks. Stratigraphers still use the two main principles established by the late 18th-century English engineer and surveyor William Smith, regarded as the father of stratigraphy: that younger beds rest upon older ones and different sedimentary beds contain different and distinctive fossils, enabling beds with similar fossils to be correlated over large distances. Today, biostratigraphy uses fossils to characterize successive intervals of geologic time, but as relatively precise time markers only to the beginning of the Cambrian Period, about 542 million years ago. The geologic time scale, back to the oldest rocks, can be quantified by isotopic dating techniques. This is the science of geochronology, which in recent years has revolutionized scientific perception of Earth history and which relies heavily on the measured parent-to-daughter ratio of radiogenic isotopes.

Paleontology is the study of fossils and is concerned not only with their description and classification, but also with an analysis of the evolution of the organisms involved. Simple fossil forms can be found in early Precambrian rocks as old as 3.5 billion years, and it is widely considered that life on Earth must have begun before the appearance of the oldest rocks. Paleontological research of the fossil record since the Cambrian Period has contributed much to the theory of evolution of life on Earth.

Several disciplines of the geologic sciences have practical benefits for society. Geologists are responsible for the discovery of minerals (such as lead, chromium, nickel, and tin), oil, gas, and coal, which are the main economic resources of Earth. They also are at the forefront of applied knowledge of subsurface structures and geologic conditions to the building industry, as well as the prevention of natural hazards or, at the very least, providing early warning of their occurrence.

Astrogeology is important in that it contributes to understanding the development of Earth within the solar system. The United States Apollo program of manned missions to the Moon, for example, provided scientists with firsthand information on lunar geology, including observations on features such as meteorite craters, which are relatively rare on Earth. Unmanned space probes have yielded significant data on the surface features of many of the planets and their satellites. Since the 1970s, even such distant planetary systems as those of Jupiter, Saturn, and Uranus have been explored by probes.

STUDY OF EARTH'S COMPOSITION

Mineralogy, petrology, economic geology, and geochemistry are disciplines nested within the field of geology. Mineralogy focuses on minerals, whereas petrology considers the rocks that contain them. Economic geology is concerned with the discovery and extraction of rocks, minerals, ores, and hydrocarbons stored beneath the surface, whereas geochemistry considers the relative abundance, distribution, and migration of Earth's chemical elements and their isotopes.

MINERALOGY

As a discipline, mineralogy has had close historical ties with geology. Minerals as basic constituents of rocks and ore deposits are obviously an integral aspect of geology. The problems and techniques of mineralogy, however, are distinct in many respects from those of the rest of geology, with the result that mineralogy has grown to be a large, complex discipline in itself.

About 3,000 distinct mineral species are recognized, but relatively few are important in the kinds of rocks that are abundant in the outer part of Earth. Thus a few minerals such as the feldspars, quartz, and mica are the essential ingredients in granite and its near relatives. Limestones, which are widely distributed on all continents, consist largely of only two minerals, calcite and dolomite. Many rocks have a more complex mineralogy, and in some the mineral particles are so minute that they can be identified only through specialized techniques.

It is possible to identify an individual mineral in a specimen by examining and testing its physical properties. Determining the hardness of a mineral is the most practical way of identifying it. This can be done by using the Mohs scale of hardness, which lists 10 common minerals in their relative order of hardness: talc (softest with the scale number 1), gypsum (2), calcite (3), fluorite (4), apatite (5), orthoclase (6), quartz (7), topaz (8), corundum (9), and diamond (10). Harder minerals scratch softer ones, so that an unknown mineral can be readily positioned between minerals on the scale. Certain common objects that have been assigned hardness values roughly corresponding to those of the Mohs scale (e.g., fingernail [2.5], pocketknife blade [5.5], steel file [6.5]) are usually used in conjunction with the minerals on the scale for additional reference.

Other physical properties of minerals that aid in identification are crystal form, cleavage type, fracture, streak, lustre, colour, specific gravity, and density. In addition, the refractive index of a mineral can be determined with precisely calibrated immersion oils. Some minerals have distinctive properties that help to identify them. For example, carbonate minerals effervesce with dilute acids, halite is soluble in water and has a salty taste, fluorite (and about 100 other minerals) fluoresces in ultraviolet light, and uranium-bearing minerals are radioactive.

Red fluorite crystals (left) *on display at the Natural History Museum in Paris. Fluorite is one of several minerals noted for its fluorescent properties, meaning it emits radiant light.* Patrick Kovarik/AFP/Getty Images

The science of crystallography is concerned with the geometric properties and internal structure of crystals. Because minerals are generally crystalline, crystallography is an essential aspect of mineralogy. Investigators in the field may use a reflecting goniometer that measures angles between crystal faces to help determine the crystal system to which a mineral belongs. Another instrument that they frequently employ is the X-ray diffractometer, which makes use of the fact that X-rays, when passing through a mineral specimen, are diffracted at regular angles. The paths of the diffracted rays are recorded on photographic film, and the positions and intensities of the resulting diffraction lines on the film provide a particular pattern. Every mineral has its own unique diffraction pattern, so crystallographers are able to determine not only the crystal structure of a mineral but the type of mineral as well.

When a complex substance such as a magma crystallizes to form igneous rock, the grains of different constituent minerals grow together and mutually interfere, with the result that they do not retain their externally recognizable crystal form. To study the minerals in such a rock, the mineralogist uses a petrographic microscope constructed for viewing thin sections of the rock, which are ground uniformly to a thickness of about 0.03 mm (0.001 inch), in light polarized by two polarizing prisms in the microscope. If the rock is crystalline, its essential minerals can be determined by their peculiar optical properties as revealed in transmitted light under magnification, provided that the individual crystal grains can be distinguished. Opaque minerals, such as those with a high content of metallic elements, require a technique employing reflected light from polished surfaces. This kind of microscopic analysis has particular application to metallic ore minerals. The polarizing microscope, however, has a lower limit to the size of grains that can be distinguished with the eye; even the best microscopes cannot resolve grains less than about 0.5 micrometre (0.0005 mm [0.00002 inch]) in diameter. For higher magnifications the mineralogist uses an electron microscope, which produces images with diameters enlarged tens of thousands of times.

The methods described above are based on a study of the physical properties of minerals. Another important area of mineralogy is concerned with the chemical composition of minerals. The primary instrument used is the electron microprobe. Here, a beam of electrons is focused on a thin section of rock that has been highly polished and coated with carbon. The electron beam can be narrowed to a diameter of about one micrometre and thus can be focused on a single grain of a mineral, which can be observed with an ordinary optical-microscope system. The electrons cause the atoms in the mineral under examination to emit diagnostic X rays, the intensity and concentration of which are measured by a computer. Besides spot analysis, this method allows a mineral to be traversed for possible chemical zoning. Moreover, the concentration and relative distribution of elements such as magnesium and iron across the boundary of two coexisting minerals like garnet and pyroxene can be used with thermodynamic data to calculate the temperature and pressure at which minerals of this type crystallize.

Although the major concern of mineralogy is to describe and classify the geometrical, chemical, and physical properties of minerals, it is also concerned with their origin. Physical chemistry and thermodynamics are basic tools for understanding mineral origin. Some of the observational data of mineralogy are concerned with the behaviour of solutions in precipitating crystalline materials under controlled conditions in the laboratory. Certain minerals can be created synthetically under conditions in which temperature and concentration of solutions are carefully monitored. Other experimental methods include study of the transformation of solids at high temperatures and pressures to yield specific minerals or assemblages of minerals. Experimental data obtained in the laboratory, coupled with chemical and physical theory, enable the conditions of origin of many naturally occurring minerals to be inferred.

PETROLOGY

Petrology is the study of rocks, and, because most rocks are composed of minerals, petrology is strongly dependent on mineralogy. In many respects mineralogy and petrology share the same problems; for example, the physical conditions that prevail (pressure, temperature, time, and presence or absence of water) when particular minerals or mineral assemblages are formed. Although petrology is in principle concerned with rocks throughout the crust, as well as with those of the inner depths of Earth, in practice the discipline deals mainly with those that are accessible in the outer part of Earth's crust. Rock specimens obtained from the surface of the Moon and from other planets are also proper considerations of petrology. Fields of specialization in petrology correspond to the aforementioned three major rock types—igneous, sedimentary, and metamorphic.

IGNEOUS PETROLOGY

Igneous petrology is concerned with the identification, classification, origin, evolution, and processes of formation and crystallization of the igneous rocks. Most of the rocks available for study come from Earth's crust, but a few, such as eclogites, derive from the mantle. The scope of igneous petrology is very large because igneous rocks make up the bulk of the continental and oceanic crusts and of the mountain belts of the world, which range in age from early Archean to Neogene, and they also include the high-level volcanic extrusive rocks and the plutonic rocks that formed deep within the crust.

Of utmost importance to igneous petrologic research is geochemistry, which is concerned with the major- and trace-element composition of igneous rocks as well as of the magmas from which they arose. Some of the major problems within the scope of igneous petrology are: (1) the form and structure of igneous bodies, whether they be lava flows or granitic intrusions, and their relations to surrounding rocks (these are problems studied in the field); (2) the crystallization history of the minerals that make up igneous rocks (this is determined with the petrographic polarizing microscope); (3) the classification of rocks based on textural features, grain size, and the abundance and composition of constituent minerals; (4) the fractionation of parent magmas by the process of magmatic differentiation, which may give rise to an evolutionary sequence of genetically related igneous products; (5) the mechanism of generation of magmas by partial melting of the lower continental crust, suboceanic and subcontinental mantle, and subducting slabs of oceanic lithosphere; (6) the history of formation and the composition of the present oceanic crust determined on the basis of data from the Integrated Ocean Drilling Program (IODP); (7) the evolution of igneous rocks through geologic time; (8) the composition of the mantle from studies of the rocks and mineral chemistry of eclogites brought to the surface in kimberlite pipes; (9) the conditions of pressure and temperature at which different magmas form and at which their igneous products crystallize (determined from high-pressure experimental petrology).

The basic instrument of igneous petrology is the petrographic polarizing microscope, but the majority of instruments used today have to do with determining rock and mineral chemistry. These include the X-ray fluorescence spectrometer, equipment for neutron activation analysis, induction-coupled plasma spectrometer, electron microprobe, ionprobe, and mass spectrometer. These instruments are highly computerized and automatic and produce analyses rapidly. Complex high-pressure experimental laboratories also provide vital data.

With a vast array of sophisticated instruments available, the igneous petrologist is able to answer many fundamental questions. Study of the ocean floor has been combined with investigation of ophiolite complexes, which are interpreted as slabs of ocean floor that have been thrust onto adjacent continental margins. An ophiolite provides a much deeper section through the ocean floor than is available from shallow drill cores and dredge samples from the extant ocean floor. These studies have shown that the topmost volcanic layer consists of tholei-itic basalt or mid-ocean ridge basalt that crystallized at an accreting rift or ridge in the middle of an ocean. A combination of mineral chemistry of the basalt minerals and experimental petrology of such phases allows investigators to calculate the depth and temperature of the magma chambers along the mid-ocean ridge. The depths are close to 6 km (about 4 miles), and the temperatures range from 1,150 to 1,279 °C (2,102–2,334 °F). Comprehensive petrologic investigation of all the layers in an ophiolite makes it possible to determine the structure and evolution of the associated magma chamber.

In 1974 B.W. Chappell and A.J.R. White discovered two major and distinct types of granitic rock—namely, I- and S-type granitoids. The I-type has strontium-87/strontium-86 ratios lower than 0.706 and contains magnetite, titanite, and allanite but no muscovite. These rocks formed above subduction zones in island arcs and active (subducting) continental margins and were ultimately derived by partial melting of mantle and subducted oceanic lithosphere. In contrast, S-type granitoids have strontium-87/strontium-86 ratios higher than 0.706 and contain muscovite, ilmenite, and monazite. These rocks were formed by partial melting of lower continental crust. Those found in the Himalayas were formed during the Miocene Epoch some 20 million years ago as a result of the penetration of India into Asia, which thickened the continental crust and then caused its partial melting.

In the island arcs and active continental margins that rim the Pacific Ocean, there are many different volcanic and plutonic rocks belonging to the calc-alkaline series. These include basalt; andesite; dacite; rhyolite; ignimbrite; diorite; granite; peridotite; gabbro; and tonalite, trondhjemite, and granodiorite (TTG). They occur typically in vast batholiths, which may reach several thousand kilometres in length and contain more than 1,000 separate granitic bodies. These TTG calc-alkaline rocks represent the principal means of growth of the continental crust throughout the whole of geologic time. Much research is devoted to them in an effort to determine the source regions of their parent magmas and the chemical evolution of the magmas. It is generally agreed that these magmas were largely derived by the melting of a subducted oceanic slab and the overlying hydrated mantle wedge. One of the major influences on the evolution of these rocks is the presence of water, which was derived originally from the dehydration of the subducted slab.

SEDIMENTARY PETROLOGY

The field of sedimentary petrology is concerned with the description and classification of sedimentary rocks, interpretation of the processes of transportation and deposition of the sedimentary materials forming the rocks, the environment that prevailed at the time the sediments were deposited, and the alteration (compaction, cementation, and chemical and mineralogical modification) of the sediments after deposition.

There are two main branches of sedimentary petrology. One branch deals with carbonate rocks, namely limestones and dolomites, composed principally of calcium carbonate (calcite) and calcium magnesium carbonate (dolomite). Much of the complexity in classifying carbonate rocks stems partly from the fact that many limestones and dolomites have been formed, directly or indirectly, through the influence of organisms, including bacteria, lime-secreting algae, various shelled organisms (e.g., mollusks and brachiopods), and by corals. In limestones and dolomites that were deposited under marine conditions, commonly in shallow warm seas, much of the material initially forming the rock consists of skeletons of lime-secreting organisms. In many examples, this skeletal material is preserved as fossils. Some of the major problems of carbonate petrology concern the physical and biological conditions of the environments in which carbonate material has been deposited, including water depth, temperature, degree of illumination by sunlight, motion by waves and currents, and the salinity and other chemical aspects of the water in which deposition occurred.

The other principal branch of sedimentary petrology is concerned with the sediments and sedimentary rocks that are essentially noncalcareous. These include sands and sandstones, clays and claystones, siltstones, conglomerates, glacial till, and varieties of sandstones, siltstones, and conglomerates (e.g., the graywacke-type sandstones and siltstones). These rocks are broadly known as clastic rocks because they consist of distinct particles or clasts. Clastic petrology is concerned with classification, particularly with respect to the mineral composition of fragments or particles, as well as the shapes of particles (angular versus rounded), and the degree of homogeneity of particle sizes. Other main concerns of clastic petrology are the mode of transportation of sedimentary materials, including the transportation of clay, silt, and fine sand by wind, and the transportation of these and coarser materials through suspension in water, through traction by waves and currents in rivers, lakes, and seas, and sediment transport by ice.

Sedimentary petrology also is concerned with the small-scale structural features of sediments and sedimentary rocks. Features that can be conveniently seen in a specimen held in the hand are within the domain of sedimentary petrology. These features include the geometrical attitude of mineral grains with respect to each other, small-scale cross stratification, the shapes and interconnections of pore spaces, and the presence of fractures and veinlets.

Instruments and methods used by sedimentary petrologists include the petrographic microscope for description and classification, X-ray mineralogy for defining fabrics and small-scale structures, physical model flume experiments for studying the effects of flow as an agent of transport and the development of sedimentary structures, and mass spectrometry for calculating stable isotopes and the temperatures of deposition, cementation, and diagenesis. Wet-suit diving permits direct observation of current processes on coral reefs, and manned submersibles enable observation at depth on the ocean floor and in mid-oceanic ridges.

The plate-tectonic theory has given rise to much interest in the relationships between sedimentation and tectonics, particularly in modern plate-tectonic environments — e.g., spreading-related settings (intracontinental

Scientists conducting an experiment near the ocean floor. Deep sea diving allows petrologists to observe conditions that affect oceanic sedimentary rock. Brian Skerry/National Geographic Image Collection/Getty Images

rifts, early stages of intercontinental rifting such as the Red Sea, and late stages of intercontinental rifting such as the margins of the present Atlantic Ocean), mid-oceanic settings (ridges and transform faults), subduction-related settings (volcanic arcs, fore-arcs, back-arcs, and trenches), and continental collision-related settings (the Alpine-Himalayan belt and late orogenic basins with molasse [i.e., thick association of clastic sedimentary rocks consisting chiefly of sandstones and shales]). Today, many subdisciplines of sedimentary petrology are concerned with the detailed investigation of the various sedimentary processes that occur within these plate-tectonic environments.

METAMORPHIC PETROLOGY

Metamorphism means change in form. In geology the term is used to refer to a solid-state recrystallization of earlier igneous, sedimentary, or metamorphic rocks. There are two main types of metamorphism: (1) contact metamorphism, in which changes induced largely by increase in temperature are localized at the contacts of igneous intrusions; and (2) regional metamorphism, in which increased pressure and temperature have caused recrystallization over extensive regions in mountain belts. Other types of metamorphism include local effects caused by deformation in fault zones, burning oil shales, and thrusted ophiolite complexes; extensive recrystallization caused by high heat flow in mid-ocean ridges; and shock metamorphism induced by high-pressure impacts of meteorites in craters on Earth and the Moon.

Metamorphic petrology is concerned with field relations and local tectonic environments; the description and classification of metamorphic rocks in terms of their texture and chemistry, which provides information on the nature of the premetamorphic material; the study of minerals and their chemistry (the mineral assemblages and their possible reactions), which yields data on the temperatures and pressures at which the rocks recrystallized; and the study of fabrics and the relations of mineral growth to deformation stages and major structures, which provides information about the tectonic conditions under which regional metamorphic rocks formed.

A supplement to metamorphism is metasomatism: the introduction and expulsion of fluids and elements through rocks during recrystallization. When new crust is formed and metamorphosed at a mid-oceanic ridge, seawater penetrates into the crust for a few kilometres and carries much sodium with it. During formation of a contact metamorphic aureole around a granitic intrusion, hydrothermal fluids carrying elements such as iron, boron, and fluorine pass from the granite into the wall rocks. When the continental crust is thickened, its lower part may suffer dehydration and form granulites. The expelled fluids, carrying such heat-producing elements as rubidium, uranium, and thorium, migrate upward into the upper crust. Much petrologic research is concerned with determining the amount and composition of fluids that have passed through rocks during these metamorphic processes.

The basic instrument used by the metamorphic petrologist is the petrographic microscope, which allows detailed study and definition of mineral types, assemblages, and reactions. If a heating/freezing stage is attached to the microscope, the temperature of formation and composition of fluid inclusions within minerals can be calculated. These inclusions are remnants of the fluids that passed through the rocks during the final stages of their recrystallization. The electron microprobe is widely used for analyzing the composition of the component minerals. The petrologist can combine the mineral chemistry with data from experimental studies and thermodynamics to calculate the pressures and temperatures at which the rocks recrystallized. By obtaining information on the isotopic age of successive metamorphic events with a mass spectrometer, pressure–temperature–time curves can be worked out.

These curves chart the movement of rocks over time as they were brought to the surface from deep within the continental crust. This technique is important for understanding metamorphic processes. Some continental metamorphic rocks that contain diamonds and coesites (ultrahigh pressure minerals) have been carried down subduction zones to a depth of at least 100 km (60 miles), brought up, and often exposed at the present surface within resistant eclogites of collisional orogenic belts— such as the Swiss Alps, the Himalayas, the Kokchetav metamorphic terrane in Kazakhstan, and the Variscan belt in Germany. These examples demonstrate that metamorphic petrology plays a key role in unraveling tectonic processes in mountain belts that have passed through the plate-tectonic cycle of events.

ECONOMIC GEOLOGY

The mineral commodities on which modern civilization is heavily dependent are obtained from Earth's crust and have a prominent place in the study and practice of economic geology. In turn, economic geology consists of several principal branches that include the study of ore deposits, petroleum geology, and the geology of nonmetallic deposits (excluding petroleum), such as coal, stone, salt, gypsum, clay and sand, and other commercially valuable materials.

The practice of economic geology is distinguished by the fact that its objectives are to aid in the exploration for and extraction of mineral resources. The objectives are therefore economic. In petroleum geology, for example, a common goal is to guide oil-well-drilling programs so that the most profitable prospects are drilled, and those that are likely to be of marginal economic value, or barren, are avoided. A similar philosophy influences the other branches of economic geology. In this sense, economic geology can be considered as an aspect of business that is devoted to economic decision making. Many deposits of economic interest, particularly those of metallic ores, are of extreme scientific interest in themselves, however, and they have warranted intensive study that has been somewhat apart from economic considerations.

The practice of economic geology provides employment for a large number of geologists. On a worldwide basis, probably more than two-thirds of people employed in the geologic sciences are engaged in work that touches on the economic aspects of geology. These include geologists whose main interests lie in diverse fields of the geologic sciences. For example, the petroleum industry, which collectively is the largest employer of economic geologists, attracts individuals with specialties in stratigraphy, sedimentary petrology, structural geology, paleontology, and geophysics.

GEOCHEMISTRY

Geochemistry is broadly concerned with the application of chemistry to virtually all aspects of geology. Inasmuch as Earth is composed of the chemical elements, all geologic materials and most geologic processes can be regarded from a chemical point of view.

CHEMISTRY OF EARTH

Some of the major problems that broadly belong to geochemistry are as follows: the origin and abundance of the elements in the solar system, galaxy, and universe (cosmochemistry); the abundance of elements in the major divisions of Earth, including the core, mantle, crust, hydrosphere, and atmosphere; the behaviour of ions in the structure of crystals; the chemical reactions in cooling magmas and the origin and evolution of deeply buried intrusive igneous rocks; the chemistry of volcanic (extrusive) igneous rocks and of phenomena closely related to volcanic activity, including hot-spring activity, emanation of volcanic gases, and origin of ore deposits formed by hot waters derived during the late stages of cooling of igneous magmas; chemical reactions involved in weathering of rocks in which earlier formed minerals decay and new minerals are created; the transportation of weathering products in solution by natural waters in the ground and in streams, lakes, and the sea; chemical changes that accompany compaction and cementation of unconsolidated sediments to form sedimentary rocks; and the progressive chemical and mineralogical changes that take place as rocks undergo metamorphism.

One of the leading general concerns of geochemistry is the continual recycling of the materials of Earth. This process takes place in several ways It is widely believed that oceanic and continental basalts crystallized from magmas that were ultimately derived by partial melting of Earth's mantle. Much geochemical research is devoted to the quantification of this extraction of mantle material and its contribution to crustal growth throughout geologic time in the many stages of seafloor formation and mountain building. When the basalts that formed at the mid-oceanic ridge are transported across the ocean by the process of seafloor spreading, they interact with seawater, and this involves the adding of sodium to the basaltic crust and the extraction of calcium from it.

Geophysical data confirm the idea that the oceanic lithosphere is being consumed along Earth's major subduction zones below the continental lithosphere—e.g., along the continental margin of the Andes Mountain Ranges. This may involve pelagic sediments from the ocean floor, oceanic basalts altered by seawater exchange, gabbros, ultramafic rocks, and segments of the underlying mantle. Many geochemists are studying what happens to this subducted material and how it contributes to the growth of island arcs and Andean-type mountain belts.

Another way in which material is recycled involves the behaviour of dissolved materials in natural waters, under the relatively low temperatures that prevail at or near the surface of Earth. This is an integral aspect of the crustal cycle. Weathering processes supply dissolved material, including silica, calcium carbonate, and other salts, to streams. These materials then enter the oceans, where some remain in solution (e.g., sodium chloride), whereas others are progressively removed to form certain sedimentary rocks, including limestone and dolomite, and, where conditions are conducive for the formation of deposits by means of evaporation, gypsum (hydrous calcium sulfate), rock salt (halite), and potash deposits may occur.

The behaviour of biological materials and their subsequent disposition are important aspects of geochemistry, generally termed organic geochemistry and biogeochemistry. Major problems of organic geochemistry include the question of the chemical environment on Earth in which life originated; the modification of the hydrosphere, and particularly the atmosphere, through the effects of life; and the incorporation of organic materials in rocks, including carbonaceous material in sedimentary rocks. The nature and chemical transformations of biological material present in deposits of coal, petroleum, and natural gas lie within the scope of organic geochemistry. Organic chemical reactions influence many geochemical processes, as, for example, rock weathering and production of soil, the solution, precipitation, and secretion of such dissolved materials as calcium carbonate, and the alteration of sediments to form sedimentary rocks. Biogeochemistry deals chiefly with the cyclic flows of individual elements and their compounds between living and nonliving systems.

Geochemistry has applications to other subdisciplines within geology, as well as to disciplines relatively far removed from it. At one extreme, geochemistry is linked with cosmology in a number of ways. These include the study of the chemical composition of meteorites, the relative abundance of elements within Earth, the Moon, and other planets, and the ages of meteorites and of rocks of the crust of Earth and Moon as established by radiometric means. At the other extreme, the geochemistry of traces of metals in rocks and soils and, ultimately, in the food chain has important consequences for humans and for the vast body of lesser organisms on which they are dependent and with whom they coexist. Deficiencies in traces of copper and cobalt in forage plants, for example, lead to diseases in certain grazing animals and may locally influence human health. These deficiencies are in turn related to the concentrations of these elements in rocks and the manner in which they are chemically combined within soils and rocks.

The chemical analysis of minerals is undertaken with the electron microprobe. Instruments and techniques used for the chemical analysis of rocks are as follows: The X-ray fluorescent (XRF) spectrometer excites atoms with a primary X-ray beam and causes secondary (or fluorescent) X rays to be emitted. Each element produces a diagnostic X radiation, the intensity of which is measured. This intensity is proportional to the concentration of the element in the rock, and so the bulk composition can be calculated. The crushed powder of the rock is compressed into a disk or fused into a bead and loaded into the spectrometer, which analyzes it automatically under computer control. Analysis of most elements having concentrations of more than five parts per million is possible.

Neutron-activation analysis is based on the fact that certain elements are activated or become radiogenic when they are bombarded with a flux of neutrons formed from the radioactive decay of uranium-235 in a nuclear reactor. With the addition of the neutrons, the stable isotopes produce new unstable radionuclides, which then decay, emitting particles with diagnostic energies that can be separated and measured individually. The technique is particularly suitable for the analysis of the rare earth elements, uranium, thorium, barium, and hafnium, with a precision to less than one part per million.

The induction-coupled plasma (ICP) spectrometer can analyze over 40 elements. Here, a solution of a rock is put into a plasma, and the concentration of the elements is determined from the light emitted. This method is rapid, and the ICP spectrometer is particularly suited to analyzing large numbers of soil and stream sediment samples, as well as mineralized rocks in mineral exploration.

ISOTOPIC GEOCHEMISTRY

Isotopic geochemistry has several principal roles in geology. One is concerned with the enrichment or impoverishment of certain isotopic species that results from the influence of differences in mass of molecules containing different isotopes. Measurements of the proportions of various isotopic species can be used as a form of geologic thermometer. The ratio of oxygen-16 to oxygen-18 in calcium carbonate secreted by various marine organisms from calcium carbonate in solution in seawater is influenced by the temperature of the seawater. Precise measurement of the proportions of oxygen-16 with respect to oxygen-18 in calcareous shells of some fossil marine organisms provides a means of estimating the temperatures of the seas in which they lived. The varying ocean temperatures during and between the major advances of glaciers during the ice ages have been inferred by analyzing the isotopic composition of the skeletons of floating organisms recovered as fossils in sediment on the seafloor. Other uses of isotopic analyses that involve temperature-dependent rate processes include the progressive removal of crystals from cooling igneous magmas.

Another role of isotopic geochemistry that is of great importance in geology is radiometric age dating. The ability to quantify the geologic time scale—i.e., to date the events of the geologic past in terms of numbers of years—is largely a result of coupling radiometric-dating techniques with older, classical methods of establishing relative geologic ages. As explained earlier, radiometric-dating methods are based on the general principle that a particular radioactive isotope (radioactive parent or source material) incorporated in geologic material decays at a uniform rate, producing a decay product, or daughter isotope. Some radiometric "clocks" are based on the ratio of the proportion of parent to daughter isotopes, others on the proportion of parent remaining, and still others on the proportion of daughter isotopes with respect to each other. For example, uranium-238 decays ultimately to lead-206, which is one of the four naturally occurring isotopic species of lead. Minerals that contain uranium-238 when initially formed may be dated by measuring the proportions of lead-206 and uranium-238; the older the specimen, the greater the proportion of lead-206 with respect to uranium-238. The decay of potassium-40 to form argon-40 (calcium-40 is produced in this decay process as well) is also a widely used radiometric-dating tool, though there are several other parent-daughter pairs that are used in radiometric dating, including another isotope of uranium

(uranium-235), which decays ultimately to form lead-207, and thorium-232, which decays to lead-208.

Uranium-238 and uranium-235 decay very slowly, although uranium-235 decays more rapidly than uranium-238. The rate of decay may be expressed in several ways. One way is by the radioactive isotope's half-life — the interval of time in which half of any given initial amount will have decayed. The half-life of uranium-238 is about 4,510,000,000 years, whereas the half-life of uranium-235 is about 713,000,000 years. Other radioactive isotopes decay at greatly differing rates, with half-lives ranging from a fraction of a second to quadrillions of years.

It is useful to combine a variety of isotopic methods to determine the complete history of a crustal rock. A samarium-147–neodymium-143 date on a granitic gneiss, for example, may be interpreted as the time of mantle–crust differentiation or crustal accretion that produced the original magmatic granite. Also, a lead-207–lead-206 date on a zircon will indicate the crystallization age of the granite. In contrast, a rubidium-87–strontium-87 date of a whole rock sample may give the time at which the rock became a closed system for migration of the strontium during the period of metamorphism that converted the granite to a granitic gneiss. When potassium-40 breaks down to argon-40, the argon continues to diffuse until the rock has cooled to about 200 °C (about 400 °F); therefore, a potassium-40–argon-40 date may be interpreted as the time when the granite cooled through a blocking temperature that stopped all argon release. This may reflect the cooling of the granite during late uplift in a young mountain belt.

Since the 1980s, two technological advancements have greatly increased the geologist's ability to compute the isotopic age of rocks and minerals. The SHRIMP (Sensitive High Mass Resolution Ion Microprobe) enables the accurate determination of the uranium-lead age of the mineral zircon, and this has revolutionized the understanding of the isotopic age of formation of zircon-bearing igneous granitic rocks. Another technological development is the ICP-MS (Inductively Coupled Plasma Mass Spectrometer), which is able to provide the isotopic age of zircon, titanite, rutile, and monazite. These minerals are common to many igneous and metamorphic rocks.

Carbon-14 is a radioactive isotope of carbon (carbon-12 and carbon-13 are stable isotopes) with a half-life of 5,570 years. Carbon-14 is incorporated in all living material, for it is derived either directly or indirectly from its presence in atmospheric carbon dioxide. The moderately short half-life of carbon-14 makes it useful for dating biological materials that are more than a few hundred years old and less than 30,000 years old. It has been used to provide correlation of events within this time span, particularly those of the Pleistocene Epoch involving Earth's most recent ice ages.

STUDY OF EARTH'S STRUCTURE

The disciplines within geology that consider Earth's structure in particular include geodesy, geophysics, structural geology, tectonics, and volcanology. The scientific objective of geodesy is to determine the size and shape of Earth, whereas geophysics concentrates on studies of Earth that involve the methods and principles of physics. Structural geology deals with the geometric relationships of rocks and geologic features in general, and tectonics is concerned with Earth's large-scale structural features, such as the planet's tectonic plates. Volcanology is somewhat related to tectonics, but its focus is on volcanoes and their evolution.

GEODESY

Although issues of size and shape are at the forefront of geodesy, the practical role of the discipline is to provide a network of accurately surveyed points on Earth's surface, the vertical elevations and geographic positions of which are precisely known and, in turn, may be incorporated in maps. When two geographic coordinates of a control point on Earth's surface, its latitude and longitude, are known, as well as its elevation above sea level, the location of that point is known with an accuracy within the limits of error involved in the surveying processes. In mapping large areas, such as a whole state or country, the irregularities in Earth's curvature must be considered. A network of precisely surveyed control points provides a skeleton to which other surveys may be tied to provide progressively finer networks of more closely spaced points. The resulting networks of points have many uses, including anchor points or bench marks for surveys of highways and other civil features. A major use of control points is to provide reference points to which the contour lines and other features of topographic maps are tied. Most topographic maps are made using photogrammetric techniques and aerial photographs.

Earth's figure is that of a surface called the geoid, which over Earth is the average sea level at each location; under the continents the geoid is an imaginary continuation of sea level. The geoid is not a uniform spheroid, however, because of the existence of irregularities in the attraction of gravity from place to place on Earth's surface. These irregularities of the geoid would bring about serious errors in the surveyed location of control points if astronomical methods, which involve use of the local horizon, were used solely in determining locations. Because of these irregularities, the reference surface used in geodesy is that of a regular mathematical surface, an ellipsoid of revolution that fits the geoid as closely as possible. This reference ellipsoid is below the geoid in some places and above it in others. Over the oceans, mean sea level defines the geoid surface, but over the land areas, the geoid is an imaginary sea-level surface.

Today, perturbations in the motions of artificial satellites are used to define the global geoid and gravity pattern with a high degree of accuracy. Geodetic satellites are positioned at a height of 700–800 km (about 435–500 miles) above Earth. Simultaneous range observations from several laser stations fix the position of a satellite, and radar altimeters measure directly its height over the oceans. Results show that the geoid is irregular; in places its surface is up to 100 metres (about 330 feet) higher than the ideal reference ellipsoid and elsewhere it is as much as 100 metres below it. The most likely explanation for this height variation is that the gravity (and density) anomalies are related to mantle convection and temperature differences at depth. An important observation that confirms this interpretation is that there is a close correlation between the gravity anomalies and the surface expression of Earth's plate boundaries. This also strengthens the idea that the ultimate driving force of plate tectonics is a large-scale circulation of the mantle.

A similar satellite ranging technique is also used to determine the drift rates of continents. Repeated measurements of laser light travel times between ground stations and satellites permit the relative movement of different control blocks to be calculated.

GEOPHYSICS

The scope of geophysics touches on virtually all aspects of geology, ranging from considerations of the conditions in Earth's deep interior, where temperatures of several thousands of degrees Celsius and pressures of millions of atmospheres prevail, to Earth's exterior, including its atmosphere and hydrosphere. The study of Earth's interior provides a good example of the geophysicist's approach to problems. Direct observation is obviously impossible. Extensive knowledge of Earth's interior has been derived from a variety of measurements, however, including seismic waves produced by quakes that travel through Earth, measurements of the flow of heat from Earth's interior into the outer crust, and by astronomical and other geologic considerations.

Geophysics may be divided into a number of overlapping branches in the following way: (1) study of the variations in Earth's gravity field; (2) seismology, the study of Earth's crust and interior by analysis of the transmission of elastic waves that are reflected or refracted; (3) the physics of the outer parts of the atmosphere, with particular attention to the radiation bombardment from the Sun and from outer space, including the influence of Earth's magnetic field on radiation intercepted by the planet; (4) terrestrial electricity, which is the study of the storage and flow of electricity in the atmosphere and the solid Earth; (5) geomagnetism, the study of the source, configuration, and changes in Earth's magnetic field and the study and interpretation of the remanent magnetism in rocks induced by Earth's magnetic field when the rocks were formed (paleomagnetism); (6) the study of Earth's thermal properties, including the temperature distribution of Earth's interior and the variation in the transmission of heat from the interior to the surface; and (7) the convergence of several of the above-cited branches for the study of the large-scale tectonic structures of Earth, such as rifts, continental margins, subduction zones, mid-oceanic ridges, thrusts, and continental sutures.

Professor Anne Hofmeister is shown loading a rock sample into a laser-flash apparatus to measure the sample's thermal conductivity. Professor Randy Korotev in Department of Earth and Planetary Sciences, Washington U., St. Louis, MO.

The techniques of geophysics include measurement of Earth's gravitational field using gravimeters on land and sea and artificial satellites in space; measurement of its magnetic field with hand-held magnetometers or larger units towed behind research ships and aircraft; and seismographic measurement of subsurface structures using reflected and refracted elastic waves generated either by earthquakes or by artificial means (e.g., underground nuclear explosions or ground vibrations produced with special pistons in large trucks). Other tools and techniques of geophysics are diverse. Some involve laboratory studies of rocks and other earth materials under high pressures and elevated temperatures. The transmission of elastic waves through Earth's crust and interior is strongly influenced by the behaviour of materials under the extreme conditions at depth. Consequently, there is strong reason to attempt to simulate those conditions of elevated temperatures and pressures in the laboratory. At another extreme, data gathered by rockets and satellites yield much information about radiation flux in space and the magnetic effects of Earth and other planetary bodies, as well as providing high precision in establishing locations in geodetic surveying, particularly over the oceans. Finally, it should be emphasized that the tools of geophysics are essentially mathematical and that most geophysical concepts are necessarily expounded mathematically.

Geophysics has major influence both as a field of pure science in which the objective is pursuit of knowledge for the sake of knowledge and as an applied science in which the objectives involve solution of problems of practical or commercial interest. Its principal commercial applications lie in the exploration for oil and natural gas and, to a lesser extent, in the search for metallic ore deposits. Geophysical methods also are used in certain geologic-engineering applications, as in determining the depth of alluvial fill that overlies bedrock, which is an important factor in the construction of highways and large buildings.

Much of the success of the plate tectonics theory has depended on the corroborative factual evidence provided by geophysical techniques. For example, seismology has demonstrated that the earthquake belts of the world demarcate the plate boundaries and that intermediate and deep seismic foci define the dip of subduction zones. The study of rock magnetism has defined the magnetic anomaly patterns of the oceans, and paleomagnetism has charted the drift of continents through geologic time. Seismic reflection profiling has revolutionized scientific ideas about the deep structure of the continents. Major thrusts, such as the Wind River thrust in Wyoming and the Moine thrust in northwestern Scotland, can be seen on the profiles to extend from the surface to the Moho at about 35-km (22-mile) depth, while the Appalachian

Mountains, in the eastern United States, must have been pushed at least 260 km (about 160 miles) westward to their present position on a major thrust plane that now lies at about 15 km (about 9 miles) depth. The thick crust of Tibet can be shown to consist of a stack of major thrust units, the shape and structure of continental margins against such oceans as the Atlantic and the Pacific are beautifully illustrated on the profiles, and the detailed structure of entire sedimentary basins can be studied in the search for oil reservoirs.

STRUCTURAL GEOLOGY

The scope of structural geology is vast, ranging in size from submicroscopic lattice defects in crystals to mountain belts and plate boundaries. Structures may be divided into two broad classes: the primary structures that were acquired in the genesis of a rock mass and the secondary structures that result from later deformation of the primary structures.

Most layered rocks (sedimentary rocks, some lava flows, and pyroclastic deposits) were deposited initially as nearly horizontal layers. Rocks that were initially horizontal may be deformed later by folding and may be displaced along fractures. If displacement has occurred and the rocks on the two sides of the fracture have moved in opposite directions from each other, the fracture is termed a fault; if displacement has not occurred, the fracture is called a joint. It is clear that faults and joints are secondary structures—i.e., their relative age is younger than the rocks that they intersect, but their age may be only slightly younger. Many joints in igneous rocks, for example, were produced by contraction when the rocks cooled. On the other hand, some fractures in rocks, including igneous rocks, are related to weathering processes and expansion associated with removal of overlying load. These will have been produced long after the rocks were formed. The faults and joints referred to above are brittle structures that form as discrete fractures within otherwise undeformed rocks in cool upper levels of the crust. In contrast, ductile structures result from permanent changes throughout a wide body of deformed rock at higher temperatures and pressures in deeper crustal levels. Such structures include folds and cleavage in slate belts, foliation in gneisses, and mineral lineation in metamorphic rocks.

The methods of structural geology are diverse. At the smallest scale, lattice defects and dislocations in crystals can be studied in images enlarged several thousand times with transmission electron microscopes. Many structures can be examined microscopically, using the same general techniques employed in petrology, in which sections of rock mounted on glass slides are ground very thin and are then examined by transmitted light with polarizing microscopes. Of course, some structures can be studied in hand specimens, which were preferably oriented when collected in the field.

On a large scale, the techniques of field geology are employed. These include the preparation of geologic maps that show the areal distribution of geologic units selected for representation on the map. They also include the plotting of the orientation of such structural features as faults, joints, cleavage, small folds, and the attitude of beds with respect to three-dimensional space. A common objective is to interpret the structure at some depth below the surface. It is possible to infer with some degree of accuracy the structure beneath the surface by using information available at the surface. If geologic information from drill holes or mine openings is available, however, the configuration of rocks in the subsurface commonly may be interpreted with much greater assurance as compared with interpretations involving projection to depth based largely on information obtained at the surface. Vertical graphic sections are widely used to show the configuration of rocks beneath the surface. Balancing cross sections is an important technique in thrust belts. The lengths of individual thrust slices are added up and the total restored length is compared with the present length of the section and thus the percentage of shortening across the thrust belt can be calculated. In addition, contour maps that portray the elevation of particular layers with respect to sea level or some other datum are widely used, as are contour maps that represent thickness variations.

Strain analysis is another important technique of structural geology. Strain is change in shape. For example, by measuring the elliptical shape of deformed ooliths or concretions that must originally have been circular, it is possible to make a quantitative analysis of the strain patterns in deformed sediments. Other useful kinds of strain markers are deformed fossils, conglomerate pebbles, and vesicles. A long-term aim of such analysis is to determine the strain variations across entire segments of mountain belts. This information is expected to help geologists understand the mechanisms involved in the formation of such belts.

A combination of structural and geophysical methods are generally used to conduct field studies of the large-scale tectonic features mentioned below. Field work enables the mapping of the structures at the surface, and geophysical methods involving the study of seismic activity, magnetism, and gravity make possible the determination of the subsurface structures.

The processes that affect geologic structures rarely can be observed directly. The nature of the deforming forces and the manner in which Earth's materials deform under stress can be studied experimentally and theoretically, however, thus providing insight into the forces of nature. One form of laboratory experimentation involves the deformation of small, cylindrical specimens of rocks under very high pressures. Other experimental methods include the use of scale models of folds and faults consisting of soft, layered materials, in which the objective is to simulate the behaviour of real strata that have undergone deformation on a larger scale over much longer time.

Some experiments measure the main physical variables that control rock deformation—namely, temperature, pressure, deformation rate, and the presence of fluids such as water. These variables are responsible for changing the rheology of rocks from rigid and brittle at or near Earth's surface to weak and ductile at great depths. Thus experimental studies aim to define the conditions under which deformation occurs throughout Earth's crust.

TECTONICS

Tectonics forms a multidisciplinary framework for interrelating many other geologic disciplines, and thus it provides an integrated understanding of large-scale processes that have shaped the development of our planet. These structural features include mid-oceanic rifts; transform faults in the oceans; intracontinental rifts, as in the East African Rift System and on the Tibetan Highlands; wrench faults (e.g., the San Andreas Fault in California) that may extend hundreds of kilometres; sedimentary basins (oil potential); thrusts, such as the Main Central thrust in the Himalayas, that measure more than 2,000 km (about 1,240 miles) long; ophiolite complexes; passive continental margins, as around the Atlantic Ocean; active continental margins, as around the Pacific Ocean; trench systems at the mouth of subduction zones; granitic batholiths (e.g., those in Sierra

Nevada and Peru) that may be as long as 1,000 km (about 620 miles); sutures between collided continental blocks; and complete sections of mountain belts, such as the Andes, the Rockies, the Alps, the Himalayas, the Urals, and the Appalachians–Caledonians. Viewed as a whole, the study of these large-scale features encompasses the geology of plate tectonics and of mountain building at the margins of or within continents.

VOLCANOLOGY

Volcanology is the science of volcanoes and deals with their structure, petrology, and origin. It is also concerned with the contribution of volcanoes to the development of Earth's crust, with their role as contributors to the atmosphere and hydrosphere and to the balance of chemical elements in Earth's crust, and with the relationships of volcanoes to certain forms of metallic ore deposits.

Many of the problems of volcanology are closely related to those of the origin of oceans and continents. Most of the volcanoes of the world are aligned along or close to the major plate boundaries, in particular the mid-oceanic ridges and active continental margins (e.g., the "ring of fire" around the Pacific Ocean). A few volcanoes occur within oceanic plates (e.g., along the Hawaiian chain); these are interpreted as the tracks of plumes (ascending jets of partially molten mantle material) that formed when such a plate moved over hot spots fixed in the mantle.

One of the principal reasons for studying volcanoes and volcanic products is that the atmosphere and hydrosphere are believed to be largely derived from volcanic emanations, modified by biological processes. Much of the water present at Earth's surface, which has aggregated mostly in the oceans but to a lesser extent in glaciers, streams, lakes, and groundwater, probably has emerged gradually from Earth's interior by means of volcanoes, beginning very early in Earth's history. The principal components of air—nitrogen and oxygen—probably have been derived through modification of ammonia and carbon dioxide emitted by volcanoes. Emissions of vapours and gases from volcanoes are an aspect of the degassing of Earth's interior. Although the degassing processes that affect Earth were probably much more vigorous when it was newly formed about 4.6 billion years ago, it is interesting to consider that the degassing processes are still at work. Their scale, however, is vastly reduced compared with their former intensity.

The study of volcanoes is dependent on a variety of techniques. The petrologic polarizing microscope is used for classifying lava types and for tracing their general mineralogical history. The X-ray fluorescence spectrometer provides a tool for making chemical analyses of rocks that are important for understanding the chemistry of a wide variety of volcanic products (e.g., ashes, pumice, scoriae, and bombs) and of the magmas that give rise to them. Some lavas are enriched or depleted in certain isotopic ratios that can be determined with a mass spectrometer. Analyses of gases from volcanoes and of hot springs in volcanic regions provide information about the late stages of volcanic activity. These late stages are characterized by the emission of volatile materials, including sulfurous gases. Many commercially valuable ore deposits have formed through the influence of hydrothermal volcanic solutions.

Volcanoes may pose a serious hazard to human life and property, as borne out by the destruction wrought by the eruptions of Mount Vesuvius (79 CE), Krakatoa (1883), Mount Pelée (1902), and Mount Saint Helens (1980), to mention only a few. Because of this, much attention has been devoted to forecasting volcanic outbursts. In 1959

A steam cloud erupts from a volcano. Volcanology examines whether the components that make up Earth's hydrosphere and atmosphere truly have derived from volcanic gasses and vapours. Shutterstock.com

researchers monitored activity leading up to the eruption of Kilauea in Hawaii. Using seismographs, they detected swarms of earthquake tremors for several months prior to the eruption, noting a sharp increase in the number and intensity of small quakes shortly before the outpouring of lava. Tracking such tremors, which are generated by the upward movement of magma from the asthenosphere, has proved to be an effective means of determining the onset of eruptions and is now widely used for prediction purposes. Some volcanoes inflate when rising molten rock fills their magma chambers, and in such cases tiltmeters can be employed to detect a change in angle of the slope before eruption. Other methods of predicting violent volcanic activity involve the use of laser beams to check for changes in slope, temperature monitors, gas detectors, and instruments sensitive to variations in magnetic and gravity fields. Permanent volcano observatories have been established at some of the world's most active sites (e.g., Kilauea, Mount Etna, and Mount Saint Helens) to ensure early warning.

STUDY OF EARTH'S SURFACE FEATURES AND PROCESSES

Geomorphology and glacial geology are disciplines that consider the forces that shape Earth's surface features. Geomorphology is literally the study of the form or shape of Earth, but it deals principally with the topographical features of Earth's surface. Glacial geology is concerned with the properties of glaciers themselves as well as with the effects of glaciers as agents of both erosion and deposition. As such, glacial geology can be regarded as a branch of geomorphology, though it is such a large area of research that it stands as a distinct subdiscipline within the geologic sciences.

GEOMORPHOLOGY

Geomorphology is concerned with the classification, description, and origin of landforms. The configuration of Earth's surface reflects to some degree virtually all of the processes that take place at or close to the surface as well as those that occur deep in the crust. The intricate details of the shape of a mountain range, for example, result more or less directly from the processes of erosion that progressively remove material from the range. The spectrum of erosive processes includes weathering and soil-forming processes and transportation of materials by running water, wind action, and mass movement. Glacial processes have been particularly influential in many mountainous regions. These processes are destructional in the sense that they modify and gradually destroy the previous form of the range. Also important in governing the external shape of the range are the constructional processes that are responsible for uplift of the mass of rock from which the range has been sculptured. A volcanic cone, for example, may be created by the successive outpouring of lava, perhaps coupled with intermittent ejection of volcanic ash and tuff. If the cone has been built up rapidly, so that there has been relatively little time for erosive processes to modify its form, its shape is governed chiefly by the constructional processes involved in the outpouring of volcanic material. But the forces of erosion begin to modify the shape of a volcanic landform almost immediately and continue indefinitely. Thus, at no time can its shape be regarded as purely constructional or purely destructional, for its shape is necessarily a consequence of the interplay of these two major classes of processes.

Investigating the processes that influence landforms is an important aspect of geomorphology. These processes include the weathering caused by the action of solutions of atmospheric carbon dioxide and oxygen in water on exposed rocks; the activity of streams and lakes; the transport and deposition of dust and sand by wind; the movement of material through downhill creep of soil and rock and by landslides and mudflows; and shoreline processes that involve the mechanics and effects of waves and currents. Study of these different types of processes forms subdisciplines that exist more or less in their own right.

GLACIAL GEOLOGY

The important questions of glacial geology concern the climatic controls that influence the occurrence of glaciers—that is, accumulations of snow transformed into solid ice, the processes by which snow becomes ice, and

GIS

A geographic information system (GIS) is a computer system for performing geographical analysis. GIS has four interactive components: an input subsystem for converting into digital form (digitizing) maps and other spatial data; a storage and retrieval subsystem; an analysis subsystem; and an output subsystem for producing maps, tables, and answers to geographic queries. GIS is frequently used by environmental and urban planners, marketing researchers, retail site analysts, water resource specialists, and other professionals whose work relies on maps.

The two most common computer graphic formats are vector and raster, both of which are used to store graphic map elements. Vector-based GIS represents the locations of point entities as coordinate pairs in geographic space, lines as multiple points, and areas as multiple lines. Topographic surfaces are frequently represented in vector format as a series of nonoverlapping triangles, each representing a uniform slope. This representation is known as Triangulated Irregular Network (TIN). Map descriptions are stored as tabular data with pointers back to the entities. This allows the GIS to store more than one set of descriptions for each graphic map object.

Raster-based GIS represents points as individual, uniform chunks of Earth, usually squares, called grid cells. Collections of grid cells represent lines and areas. Surfaces are stored in raster format as a matrix of point elevation values, one for each grid cell, in a format known as a digital elevation model (DEM). DEM data can be converted to TIN models if needed. Whether raster or vector, the data are stored as a collection of thematic maps, variously referred to as layers, themes, or coverages.

Computer algorithms enable the GIS operator to manipulate data within a single thematic map. The GIS user may also compare and overlay data from multiple thematic maps, just as planners used to do by hand in the mid-1900s. A GIS can also find optimal routes, locate the best sites for businesses, establish service areas, create line-of-sight maps called viewsheds, and perform a wide range of other statistical and cartographic manipulations. GIS operators often combine analytical operations into map-based models through a process called cartographic modeling. Experienced GIS users devise highly sophisticated models to simulate a wide range of geographic problem-solving tasks. Some of the most complex models represent flows, such as rush-hour traffic or moving water, that include a temporal element.

the mechanism of the flow of ice within glaciers. Other important questions involve the manner in which glaciers serve as erosive agents, not only in mountainous regions but also over large regions where great continental glaciers now extend or once existed. Much of the topography of the northern part of North America and Eurasia, for example, has been strongly influenced by glaciers. In places, bedrock has been scoured of most surficial debris. Elsewhere, deposits of glacial till mantle much of the area. Other extensive deposits include unconsolidated sediments deposited in former lakes that existed temporarily as a result of dams created by glacial ice or by glacial deposits. Many presently existing lakes are of glacial origin as, for example, the Great Lakes.

Research in glacial geology is conducted with a variety of tools. Investigators use, for example, radar techniques to determine the thickness of glaciers. In order to calculate the progressive advance or retreat of glacial masses, they ascertain the age of organic materials associated with glacial moraines by means of isotopic analyses.

Other branches of the geologic sciences are closely linked with glacial geology. In glaciated regions the problems of hydrology and hydrogeology are strongly influenced by the presence of glacial deposits. Furthermore, the suitability of glacial deposits as sites for buildings, roads, and other man-made features is influenced by the mechanical properties of the deposits and by soils formed on them.

EARTH HISTORY

One of the major objectives of geology is to establish the history of Earth from its inception to the present. The most important evidence from which geologic history can be inferred is provided by the geometric relationships of rocks with respect to each other, particularly layered rocks, or strata, the relative ages of which may be determined by applying simple principles.

HISTORICAL GEOLOGY AND STRATIGRAPHY

One of the major principles of stratigraphy is that within a sequence of layers of sedimentary rock, the oldest layer is at the base and the layers are progressively younger with ascending order in the sequence. This is termed the law of superposition and is one of the great general principles of geology. Ordinarily, beds of sedimentary rocks are deposited more or less horizontally. In some regions sedimentary strata have remained more or less horizontal long after they were deposited. Some of these sedimentary rocks were deposited in shallow seas that once extended over large areas of the present continents. In many places sedimentary rocks lie much above sea level, reflecting vertical shift of the crust relative to sea level. In regions where the rocks have been strongly deformed through folding or faulting, the original attitudes of strata may be greatly altered, and sequences of strata that were once essentially horizontal may now be steeply inclined or overturned.

Prior to the development of radiometric methods of dating rocks, the ages of rocks and other geologic features could not be expressed quantitatively, or as numbers of years, but instead were expressed solely in terms of relative ages, in which the age of a particular geologic feature could be expressed as relatively younger or older than other geologic features. The ages of different sequences of strata, for example, can be compared with each other in this manner, and their relative ages with respect to faults, igneous intrusions, and other features that exhibit crosscutting relationships can be established. Given such a network of relative ages, a chronology of events has been gradually established in which the relative time of origin of various geologic features is known. This is the main thread of historical geology—an ordered sequence of geologic events whose occurrence and relative ages have been inferred from evidence preserved in the rocks. In turn, the development of radiometric dating methods has permitted numerical estimates of age to be incorporated in the scale of geologic time.

The development of the mass spectrometer has provided researchers with a means of calculating quantitative ages for rocks throughout the whole of the geologic record. With the aid of various radiometric methods involving mass spectrometric analysis, researchers have found it possible to determine how long ago a particular sediment was deposited, when an igneous rock crystallized or when a metamorphic rock recrystallized, and even the time at which rocks in a mountain belt cooled or underwent uplift. Radiometric dating also helped geochronologists discover the vast span of geologic time. The radiometric dating of meteorites revealed that Earth, like other bodies of the solar system, is about 4.6 billion years old. In contrast, the oldest minerals (detrital zircons of Western Australia) are about 4.4 billion years old, and the oldest rocks discovered so far (the faux amphibolites located on the eastern shore of Hudson Bay in Canada) formed roughly 4.28 billion years ago. It has been established that the Precambrian time occupies seven-eighths of geologic time, but the era is still poorly understood in comparison with the Phanerozoic Eon—the span of time extending from about the beginning of the Cambrian Period to the Holocene Epoch during which complex life forms are known to have existed. The success of dating Phanerozoic time with some degree of precision has depended on the interlinking of radiometric ages with biostratigraphy, which is the correlation of strata with fossils.

PALEONTOLOGY

The geologic time scale is based principally on the relative ages of sequences of sedimentary strata. Establishing the ages of strata within a region, as well as the ages of strata in other regions and on different continents, involves stratigraphic correlation from place to place. Although correlation of strata over modest distances often can be accomplished by tracing particular beds from place to place, correlation over long distances and over the oceans almost invariably involves comparison of fossils. With

GEOLOGIC TIME

The extensive interval of time occupied by Earth's geologic history is called geologic time. It extends from about 4.6 billion years ago to the present day. It is, in effect, that segment of Earth history that is represented by and recorded in rock strata.

The geologic time scale is the "calendar" for events in Earth history. It subdivides all time since the end of Earth's formative period as a planet (nearly 4.6 billion years ago) into named units of abstract time: the latter, in descending order of duration, are eons, eras, periods, and epochs. The enumeration of these geologic time units is based on stratigraphy, which is the correlation and classification of rock strata. The fossil forms that occur in these rocks provide the chief means of establishing a geologic time scale. Because living things have undergone evolutionary changes over geologic time, particular kinds of organisms are characteristic of particular parts of the geologic record. By correlating the strata in which certain types of fossils are found, the geologic history of various regions (and of Earth as a whole) can be reconstructed. The relative geologic time scale developed from the fossil record has been numerically quantified by means of absolute dates obtained with radiometric dating methods.

rare exceptions, fossils occur only in sedimentary strata. Paleontology, which is the science of ancient life and deals with fossils, is mutually interdependent with stratigraphy and with historical geology. Paleontology also may be considered to be a branch of biology.

Organic evolution is the essential principle involved in the use of fossils for stratigraphic correlation. It incorporates progressive irreversible changes in the succession of organisms through time. A small proportion of types of organisms has undergone little or no apparent change over long intervals of geologic time, but most organisms have progressively changed, and earlier forms have become extinct and, in turn, have been succeeded by more modern forms. Organisms preserved as fossils that lived over a relatively short span of geologic time and that were geographically widespread are particularly useful for stratigraphic correlation. These fossils are indexes of relative geologic age and may be termed index fossils.

Fossils play another major role in geology because they serve as indicators of ancient environments. Specialists called paleoecologists seek to determine the environmental conditions under which a fossil organism lived and the physical and biological constraints on those conditions. Did the organism live in the seas, lakes, or bogs? In what type of biological community did it live? What was its food chain? In short, what ecological niche did the organism occupy? Because oil and natural gas only accumulate in restricted environments, paleoecology can offer useful information for fossil fuel exploration.

INVERTEBRATE PALEONTOLOGY

One of the major branches of paleontology is invertebrate paleontology, which is principally concerned with fossil marine invertebrate animals large enough to be seen with little or no magnification. The number of invertebrate fossil forms is large and includes brachiopods, pelecypods, cephalopods, gastropods, corals and other coelenterates (e.g., jellyfish), bryozoans, sponges, various arthropods (invertebrates with limbs—e.g., insects), including trilobites, echinoderms, and many other forms, some of which have no living counterparts. The invertebrates that are used as index fossils generally possess hard parts, a characteristic that has fostered their preservation as fossils. The hard parts preserved include the calcareous or chitinous shells of the brachiopods, cephalopods, pelecypods, and gastropods, the jointed exoskeletons of such arthropods as trilobites, and the calcareous skeletons of frame-building corals and bryozoans. The vast variety of organisms lacking hard parts are poorly represented in the geologic record; however, they sometimes occur as impressions or carbonized films in finely laminated sediments.

VERTEBRATE PALEONTOLOGY

Vertebrate paleontology is concerned with fossils of the vertebrates: fish, amphibians, reptiles, birds, and mammals. Although vertebrate paleontology has close ties with stratigraphy, vertebrate fossils usually have not been extensively used as index fossils for stratigraphic correlation, vertebrates generally being much larger than invertebrate fossils and consequently rarer. Fossil mammals, however, have been widely used as index fossils for correlating certain nonmarine strata deposited during the Paleogene Period (about 65.5 to 23 million years ago). Much interest in dinosaurs has arisen because of the evidence that they became extinct approximately 65.5 million years ago (at the Cretaceous-Tertiary, or Cretaceous-Paleogene, boundary) during the aftermath of a large meteorite or comet impact.

MICROPALEONTOLOGY

Micropaleontology involves the study of organisms so small that they can be observed only with the aid of a microscope. The size range of microscopic fossils, however, is immense. In most cases, the term *micropaleontology* connotes that aspect of paleontology devoted to the Ostracoda, a subclass of crustaceans that are generally less than 1 mm (0.04 inch) in length; Radiolaria, marine (typically planktonic) protozoans whose remains are common in deep ocean-floor sediments; and Foraminifera, marine protozoans that range in size from about 10 cm (4 inches) to a fraction of a millimetre.

Generally speaking, micropaleontology involves successive ranges of sizes of microscopic fossils down to

The skeletons of several Radiolarian protozoa. The skeletal remains of these microscopic creatures accumulate on the ocean floor, mixing with sediment and turning to stone. Dr. Wolf Fahrenbach/Visuals Unlimited/Getty Images

organisms that must be magnified hundreds of times or more for viewing. The study of ultrasmall fossils is perhaps the fastest growing segment of contemporary paleontology and is dependent on modern laboratory instruments, including electron microscopes. It is an important aspect of oil and natural-gas exploration. Microfossils, which are flushed up boreholes in the drilling mud, can be analyzed to determine the depositional environment of the underlying sedimentary rocks and their age. This information enables geologists to evaluate the reservoir potential of the rock (i.e., its capacity for holding gas or oil) and its depth. Ostracods and foraminifera occur in such abundance and in so many varieties and shapes that they provide the basis for a detailed classification and time division of Mesozoic and Cenozoic sediments in which oil may occur.

Filamentous and spheroidal microfossils are important in many Precambrian sediments such as chert. They occur in rocks as old as 3,500,000,000 years and are thus an important testimony of early life on Earth.

Paleobotany

Paleobotany is the study of fossil plants. The oldest widely occurring fossils are various forms of calcareous algae that apparently lived in shallow seas, although some may have lived in freshwater. Their variety is so profuse that their study forms an important branch of paleobotany. Other forms of fossil plants consist of land plants or of plants that lived in swamp forests, standing in water that was fresh or may have been brackish, such as the coal-forming swamps of the Late Carboniferous Period (from 318 million to 299 million years ago).

Palynology

Palynology is the scientific discipline concerned with the study of plant pollen and spores and certain microscopic planktonic organisms, in both living and fossil form. The field is associated with the plant sciences as well as with the geologic sciences, notably those aspects dealing with stratigraphy, historical geology, and paleontology. Accordingly, the scope of palynologic research is extremely broad, ranging from the analysis of pollen morphology with electron microscopes to the study of organic microfossils (palynomorphs) extracted from ancient coals.

As pollen and spores are produced in large numbers and dispersed over large areas by wind and water, their fossils are recoverable in statistically significant assemblages in a wide variety of sedimentary rocks. Moreover, because pollen and spores are highly resistant to decay and physical alteration, they can be studied in much the same way as the components of living plants. Identification of pollen and spore microfossils has greatly aided delineation of the geographical distribution of many plant groups from early Cambrian time (some 542 million years ago) to the present.

Important, too, is the fact that the evolutionary sequence of organisms based on the large fossil remains of plants in sedimentary rocks is recorded by the sequence of plant microfossils as well. Such microfossils are thus useful in determining geologic age and are especially important in sediments devoid of large fossils. Because of their abundance and minute size, microfossils can be extracted from small samples of rock secured in drilling operations. Palynological analysis therefore is of practical application to petroleum exploration and to other geologic research involving subsurface sediments and structures.

The phases of palynology that deal exclusively with fossils are outgrowths and extensions of techniques and principles developed in the study of peat deposits of northern Europe during the early 1900s. In such research the presence, absence, and relative abundance of the pollen of various species of trees from known depths in the bog were ascertained statistically. Inasmuch as forest composition determines the pollen types trapped on the surface of a bog at any given time, it follows that changes in the pollen content reflect regional changes in forest composition. It was established that alterations in forest makeup were induced by climatic change over the many thousands of years since glacial ice disappeared from northern Europe. A relationship was thus established between the pollen content of the peat, the age (i.e., position in the bog), and climate. Application of such findings proved invaluable in subsequent studies of ancient climate, particularly the glacial and interglacial stages of the Pleistocene Epoch (approximately 2.6 million to 11,700 years ago).

ASTROGEOLOGY

Astrogeology is concerned with the geology of the solid bodies in the solar system, such as the asteroids and the planets and their moons. Research in this field helps scientists to better understand the evolution of Earth in comparison with that of its neighbours in the solar system. This subject was once the domain of astronomers, but the advent of spacecraft has made it accessible to geologists, geophysicists, and geochemists. The success of this field of study has depended largely on the development of advanced instrumentation.

The U.S. Apollo program enabled humans to land on the Moon several times since 1969. Rocks were collected, geophysical experiments were set up on the lunar surface, and geophysical measurements were made from spacecraft. The Soyuz program of the Soviet Union also collected much geophysical data from orbiting spacecraft. The mineralogy, petrology, geochemistry, and geochronology of lunar rocks were studied in detail, and this research made it possible to work out the geochemical evolution of the Moon. The various manned and unmanned missions to the Moon resulted in many other accomplishments: for example, a lunar stratigraphy was constructed; geologic maps at a scale of 1:1,000,000 were prepared; the structure of the maria, rilles, and craters was studied; gravity profiles across the dense, lava-filled maria were produced; the distribution of heat-producing radioactive elements, such as uranium and thorium, was mapped with gamma-ray spectrometers; the Moon's internal structure was determined on the basis of seismographic records of moonquakes; the heat flow from the interior was measured; and the day and night temperatures at the surface were recorded.

Since the late 1960s, unmanned spacecraft have been sent to the neighbouring planets. Several of these probes were soft-landed on Mars and Venus. Soil scoops from the Martian surface have been chemically analyzed by an on-board X-ray fluorescence spectrometer. The radioactivity of the surface materials of both Mars and Venus has been studied with a gamma-ray detector, the isotopic composition of their atmospheres analyzed with a mass spectrometer, and their magnetic fields measured. Relief and geologic maps of Mars have been made from high-resolution photographs and topographical maps of Venus compiled from radar data transmitted by orbiting spacecraft. Photographs of Mars and Mercury show that their surfaces are studded with many meteorite craters similar to those on the Moon. Detailed studies have been made of the craters, volcanic landforms, lava flows, and rift valleys on Mars, and a simplified geologic-thermal history has been constructed for the planet.

By the mid-1980s, the United States had sent interplanetary probes past Jupiter, Saturn, and Uranus. The craft transmitted data and high-resolution photographs of these outer planetary systems, including their rings and satellites.

This research has given increased impetus to the study of tektites, meteorites, and meteorite craters on Earth. The mineralogy, geochemistry, and isotopic age of meteorites and tektites have been studied in detail. Meteorites are very old and probably originated in the asteroid belt between Mars and Jupiter, while tektites are very young and most likely formed from material ejected from terrestrial meteorite craters. Many comparative studies have been made of the development and shapes of meteorite craters on Earth, the Moon, Mars, and Mercury. Space exploration has given birth to a new science—the geology of the solar system. Earth can now be understood within the framework of planetary evolution.

PRACTICAL APPLICATIONS

Advances in geological research through the years have led to a greater scientific understanding of Earth history, the forces and processes that affect its surface and subsurface regions, and the planet's place in the universe. The practical applications to this scientific knowledge are many. Geological research provides industry with the scientific tools it needs to extract energy and mineral resources, and it also enables seismologists to better predict earthquakes. The knowledge gained from geological research also informs the proper siting of civil engineering projects, such as bridges, roads, and other infrastructure. It also helps in the prevention and mitigation of water and soil contamination.

EXPLORATION FOR ENERGY AND MINERAL SOURCES

Over the past century, industries have developed rapidly, populations have grown dramatically, and standards of living have improved, resulting in an ever-growing demand for energy and mineral resources. Geologists and geophysicists have led the exploration for fossil fuels (coal, oil, natural gas, etc.) and concentrations of geothermal energy, for which applications have grown in recent years. They also have played a major role in locating deposits of commercially valuable minerals.

COAL

The Industrial Revolution of the late 18th and 19th centuries was fueled by coal. Though it has been supplanted by oil and natural gas as the primary source of energy in most modern industrial nations, coal nonetheless remains an important fuel.

The U.S. Geological Survey has estimated that only about 2 percent of the world's minable coal has so far been exploited; known reserves should last for at least 300 to 400 years. Moreover, new coal basins continue to be found, as, for example, the lignite basin discovered in the mid-1980s in Rājasthān in northwestern India.

Coal-exploration geologists have found that coal was formed in two different tectonic settings: (1) swampy marine deltas on stable continental margins, and (2) swampy freshwater lakes in graben (long, narrow troughs between two parallel normal faults) on continental crust. Knowing this and the types of sedimentary rock formations that commonly include coal, geologists can quite readily locate coal-bearing areas. Their main concern, therefore, is the quality of the coal and the thickness of the coal bed or seam. Such information can be derived from samples obtained by drilling into the rock formation in which the coal occurs.

OIL AND NATURAL GAS

During the last half of the 20th century, the consumption of petroleum products increased sharply. This has led to a depletion of many existing oil fields, notably in the United States, and intensive efforts to find new deposits.

Crude oil and natural gas in commercial quantities are generally found in sedimentary rocks along rifted continental margins and in intracontinental basins. Such environments exhibit the particular combination of geologic conditions and rock types and structures conducive to the formation and accumulation of liquid and gaseous hydrocarbons. They contain suitable source rocks (organically rich sedimentary rocks such as black shale), reservoir rocks (those of high porosity and permeability capable of holding the oil and gas that migrate into them), and overlying impermeable rocks that prevent the further upward movement of the fluids. These so-called cap rocks form petroleum traps, which may be either structural or stratigraphic depending on whether they were produced by crustal deformation or original sedimentation patterns.

Petroleum geologists concentrate their search for oil deposits in such geologic settings, mapping both the surface and subsurface features of a promising area in great detail. Geologic surface maps show subcropping sedimentary rocks and features associated with structural traps such as ridges formed by anticlines during the early stages of folding and lineations produced by fault ruptures. Maps of this kind may be based on direct observation or may be constructed with photographs taken from aircraft and Earth-orbiting satellites, particularly of terrain in remote areas. Subsurface maps reveal possible hidden underground structures and lateral variations in sedimentary rock bodies that might form a petroleum trap. The presence of such features can be detected by various means, including gravity measurements, seismic methods, and the analysis of borehole samples from exploratory drilling.

Another method used by petroleum geologists in exploratory areas involves the sampling of surface waters from swamps, streams, or lakes. The water samples are analyzed for traces of hydrocarbons, the presence of which would indicate seepage from a subsurface petroleum trap. This geochemical technique, along with seismic profiling, is often used to search for offshore petroleum accumulations.

Once an oil deposit has actually been located and well drilling is under way, petroleum geologists can determine from core samples the depth and thickness of the reservoir rock as well as its porosity and permeability. Such information enables them to estimate the quantity of the oil present and the ease with which it can be recovered.

A scientist collects a stream water sample. Petroleum geologists can tell from surface water samples whether or not deposits of fossil fuels can be found in river and lake beds. Chris Sattlberger/Photodisc/Getty Images

Although only about 15 percent of the world's oil has been exploited, petroleum geologists estimate that at the present rate of demand the supply of recoverable oil will last no more than 100 years. Owing to this rapid depletion of conventional oil sources, economic geologists have explored oil shales and tar sands as potential supplementary petroleum resources. Extracting oil from these substances is, however, very expensive and energy-intensive. In addition, the extraction process (mining and chemical treatment) poses environmental challenges, especially in regions where it occurs. Even so, oil shales and tar sands are abundant, and advances in recovery technology may yet make them attractive alternative energy resources.

GEOTHERMAL ENERGY

Another alternate energy resource is the heat from Earth's interior. The surface expression of this energy is manifested in volcanoes, fumaroles, steam geysers, hot springs, and boiling mud pools. Global heat-flow maps constructed from geophysical data show that the zones of highest heat flow occur along the active plate boundaries. There is, in effect, a close association between geothermal energy sources and volcanically active regions.

A variety of applications have been developed for geothermal energy. For example, public buildings, residential dwellings, and greenhouses in such areas as Reykjavík,

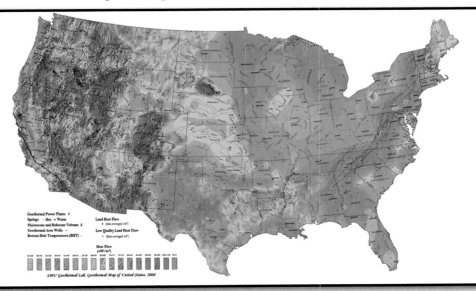

A geothermal map of the United States, 2004. Maps such as this help scientists pinpoint where to drill geothermal energy wells. Blackwell, D.D., and M. Richards, 2004. Subset of the Geothermal Map of North America. Amer. Assoc. Petroleum Geologists, Tulsa, OK. Scale 1:6,500,000.

Ice., are heated with water pumped from hot springs and geothermal wells. Hot water from such sources also is used for heating soil to increase crop production (e.g., in Oregon) and for seasoning lumber (e.g., in parts of New Zealand). The most significant application of geothermal energy, however, is the generation of electricity. The first geothermal power station began operation in Larderello,

Italy, in the early 1900s. Since then similar facilities have been built in various countries, including Iceland, Japan, Mexico, New Zealand, Turkey, the Tibet Autonomous Region of China, and the United States. In most cases turbines are driven with steam separated from superheated water tapped from underground geothermal reservoirs and geysers.

MINERAL DEPOSITS

As was mentioned above, the distribution of commercially significant mineral deposits, the economic factors associated with their recovery, and the estimates of available reserves constitute the basic concerns of economic geologists. Because continued industrial development is heavily dependent on mineral resources, their work is crucial to modern society.

It has long been known that certain periods of Earth history were especially favourable for the concentration of specific types of minerals. Copper, zinc, nickel, and gold are important in Archean rocks; magnetite and hematite are concentrated in early Proterozoic banded-iron formations; and there are economic Proterozoic uranium reserves in conglomerates. These mineral deposits and a variety of others that developed throughout the Phanerozoic Eon can be related to specific types of plate-tectonic environments. Among the latter are copper, lead, and zinc in intracontinental rifts. An interesting discovery has been the remarkable concentrations of gold, iron, zinc, and copper in brine pools and sulfide-rich muds in the Red Sea and in the Salton Sea in southern California. In many countries copper, nickel, and chromium deposits occur in ophiolite complexes obducted onto the continents from the ocean floor; porphyry copper and molybdenum deposits are found in association with granodioritic intrusions; and tungsten and tin deposits occur in many granites. The correlation of these associations and distributions with periods of Earth history, on the one hand, and plate-tectonic settings, on the other, have enabled regional metallogenetic provinces to be defined, which have proved helpful in the search for ore deposits.

During the 20th century the exploitation of mineral deposits has been so intense that serious depletion of many resources is predicted. Mercury reserves, for example, are particularly low. To deal with this problem, it has become necessary to mine deposits having smaller and smaller workable grades, a trend well illustrated by the copper mining industry, which now extracts copper from rocks with grades as low as 0.2 percent.

Investigators have discovered a major potential metallic source on the deep ocean floor, where there are large concentrations of manganese-rich nodules along with minor amounts of copper, nickel, and cobalt. Such concentrations are especially abundant in three sections of the Pacific Ocean—the area near Hawaii, that northeast of New Zealand, and that west of Central America.

EARTHQUAKE PREDICTION AND CONTROL

No natural event is as destructive over so large an area in so short a time as an earthquake. Throughout the centuries earthquakes have been responsible not only for millions of deaths but also for tremendous damage to property and the natural landscape. If major earthquakes could be predicted, it would be possible to evacuate population centres and take other measures that could minimize the loss of life and perhaps reduce damage to property as well. For this reason earthquake prediction has become a major concern of seismologists in the United States, Russia, Japan, and China.

World seismicity patterns show that earthquakes tend to occur along active plate boundaries where there is subduction (Japan) or strike-slip motion (California) and along strike-slip faults (as in China, where they are the result of the northward migration of India into Asia). Investigators agree that much more has to be learned about the physical properties of rocks in fault zones before they are able to make use of changes in these properties to predict earthquakes, though the use of Global Positioning Systems (GPS) at satellite ground stations over the years is providing quantitative data on a millimetre scale concerning the relative movement of crustal blocks across seismic faults. Recent research has suggested that rocks may become strained shortly before an earthquake and affect such observable properties of Earth's crust as seismic wave velocity and radon concentration. Leveling surveys and tiltmeter measurements have revealed that deformation in the fault zone just prior to an earthquake may cause changes in ground level and, in certain cases, variations in groundwater level. Also, some investigators have reported changes in the electric resistivity and remanent magnetization of rocks as precursory phenomena.

Since the San Francisco earthquake of 1906, seismic activity along the nearby San Andreas Fault has been closely monitored. It has been observed that numerous semicontinuous microearthquakes have occurred along some sections of the fault. These small quakes seem to release built-up strain and thus prevent large earthquakes. By contrast, intervening sections of the fault are apparently locked and thus manifest no microshocks. Consequently, seismic strain accumulating in these locked sections is expected to be released one day in a major quake.

Seismological research includes the study of earthquakes caused by human activities, such as impounding water behind high dams, injecting fluids into deep wells, excavating mines, and detonating underground nuclear explosions. In all of these cases except for deep mining, seismologists have found that the induction mechanism most likely involves the release of elastic strain, just as with earthquakes of tectonic origin. Studies of artificially induced quakes suggest that one possible method of controlling natural earthquakes is to inject fluids into fault zones so as to release strain energy.

Seismologists have done much to explain the characteristics of ground motions recorded in earthquakes. Such information is required to predict ground motions in future earthquakes, thereby enabling engineers to design earthquake-resistant structures. The largest percentage of the deaths and property damage that result from an earthquake is attributable to the collapse of buildings, bridges, and other man-made structures during the violent shaking of the ground. An effective way of reducing the destructiveness of earthquakes, therefore, is to build structures capable of withstanding intense ground motions.

OTHER AREAS OF APPLICATION

The fields of engineering, environmental, and urban geology are broadly concerned with applying the findings of geologic studies to construction engineering and to problems of land use. The location of a bridge, for example, involves geologic considerations in selecting sites for the supporting piers. The strength of geologic materials such as rock or compacted clay that occur at the sites of the piers should be adequate to support the load placed on them. Engineering geology is concerned with the engineering properties of geologic materials, including their strength, permeability, and compactability, and with the influence of these properties on the selection of locations for buildings, roads and railroads, bridges, dams, and other major civil features.

Urban geology involves the application of engineering geology and other fields of geology to environmental problems in urban areas. Environmental geology is generally concerned with those aspects of geology that touch on the human environment. Environmental and urban geology deal in large measure with those aspects of geology that directly influence land use. These include the stability of sites for buildings and other civil features, sources of water supply (hydrogeology), contamination of waters by sewage and chemical pollutants, selection of sites for burial of refuse so as to minimize pollution by seepage, and locating the source of geologic building materials, including sand, gravel, and crushed rock. Since the late 1990s the importance of environmental geology has increased considerably in most developed countries as societies became aware of the environmental impact of humankind.

CHAPTER 3
EARTH EXPLORATION

E arth exploration is the investigation of Earth's surface and its interior. By the beginning of the 20th century most of Earth's surface had been explored, at least superficially, except for the Arctic and Antarctic regions.

Today the last of the unmarked areas on land maps have been filled in by radar and photographic mapping from aircraft and satellites. One of the last areas to be mapped was the Darién peninsula between the Panama Canal and Colombia. Heavy clouds, steady rain, and dense jungle vegetation made its exploration difficult, but airborne radar was able to penetrate the cloud cover to produce reliable, detailed maps of the area. In recent years data returned by Earth satellites have led to several notable discoveries, as, for example, drainage patterns in the Sahara, which are relics of a period when this region was not arid.

Historically, exploration of Earth's interior was confined to the near surface, and this was largely a matter of following downward those discoveries made at the surface. Most present-day scientific knowledge of the subject has been obtained through geophysical research conducted since World War II, and the deep Earth remains a major frontier in the 21st century.

Exploration of space and the ocean depths has been facilitated by the placement of sensors and related devices in these regions. Only a very limited portion of the subsurface regions of Earth, however, can be studied in this way. Investigators can drill into only the uppermost crust, and the high cost severely limits the number

Satellite image of Scoresby Sund, Greenland. Jacques Descloitres, MODIS Rapid Response Team, NASA/GSFC

of holes that can be drilled. The deepest borehole so far drilled extends only to a depth of about 10 km (6 miles). Because direct exploration is so restricted, investigators are forced to rely extensively on geophysical measurements.

PRIMARY OBJECTIVES AND ACCOMPLISHMENTS

Scientific curiosity, the desire to understand better the nature of Earth, is a major motive for exploring its surface and subsurface regions. Another key motive is the prospect of economic profit. Improved standards of living have increased the demand for water, fuel, and other materials, creating economic incentives. Pure knowledge has often been a by-product of profit-motivated exploration; by the same token, substantial economic benefits have resulted from the quest for scientific knowledge.

Many surface and subsurface exploratory projects are undertaken with the aim of locating: (1) oil, natural gas, and coal; (2) concentrations of commercially important minerals (for example, ores of iron, copper, and uranium) and deposits of building materials (sand, gravel, etc.); (3) recoverable groundwater; (4) various rock types at different depths for engineering planning; (5) geothermal reserves for heating and electricity; and (6) archaeological features.

Concern for safety has prompted extensive searches for possible hazards before major construction projects are undertaken. Sites for dams, power plants, nuclear reactors, factories, tunnels, roads, hazardous waste depositories, and so forth need to be stable and provide assurance that underlying formations will not shift or slide from the weight of the construction, move along a fault during an earthquake, or permit the seepage of water or wastes. Accordingly, prediction and control of earthquakes and volcanic eruptions are major fields of research in the United States and Japan, countries susceptible to such hazards. Geophysical surveys furnish a more complete picture than test boreholes alone, although some boreholes are usually drilled to verify the geophysical interpretation.

METHODOLOGY AND INSTRUMENTATION

Geophysical techniques involve measuring reflectivity, magnetism, gravity, acoustic or elastic waves, radioactivity, heat flow, electricity, and electromagnetism. Most measurements are made on the surface of the land or sea, but some are taken from aircraft or satellites, and still others are made underground in boreholes or mines and at ocean depths.

Geophysical mapping depends on the existence of a difference in physical properties of adjacent bodies of rock—i.e., between whatever is being sought and those of the surroundings. Often the difference is provided by something associated with but other than what is being sought. Examples include a configuration of sedimentary layers that form a trap for oil accumulation, a drainage pattern that might affect groundwater flow, or a dike or host rock where minerals may be concentrated. Different methods depend on different physical properties. Which particular method is used is determined by what is being sought. In most cases, however, data from a combination of methods rather than from simply one method yield a much clearer picture.

REMOTE SENSING

Remote sensing comprises measurements of electro-magnetic radiation from the ground, usually of reflected energy in various spectral ranges measured from aircraft or satellites. This encompasses aerial photography and other kinds of measurements that are generally displayed in the form of photographlike images. Its applications involve a broad range of studies, including cartographic, botanical, geological, and military investigations.

Remote-sensing techniques involve using a combination of images. Those taken from different flight paths can be combined to allow an interpreter to perceive features in three dimensions, while those in different spectral bands may identify specific types of rock, soil, vegetation, and other entities, where species have distinctive reflectance values in different spectral regions (i.e., tone signatures). Images taken at intervals make it possible to observe changes that occur over time, such as the seasonal growth of a crop or changes wrought by a storm or flood. Those taken at different times of the day or at different sun angles may reveal quite distinct features. For example, sea-floor features in relatively shallow water in a calm sea can be mapped when the Sun is high. Radar radiation penetrates clouds and thus permits mapping from above them. Side-looking airborne radar (SLAR) is sensitive to changes in land slope and surface roughness. By registering images from adjacent flight paths, synthetic stereo pairs may give ground elevations.

Thermal infrared energy is detected by an optical-mechanical scanner. The detector is cooled by a liquid-nitrogen (or liquid-helium) jacket that encloses it, making the instrument sensitive at long wavelengths and isolating it from heat radiation from the immediate surroundings. A rotating mirror directs radiation coming from various directions onto the sensor. An image can be created by displaying the output in a form synchronized with the direction of the beam (as with a cathode-ray tube). Infrared radiation permits mapping surface temperatures to a precision of less than a degree and thus

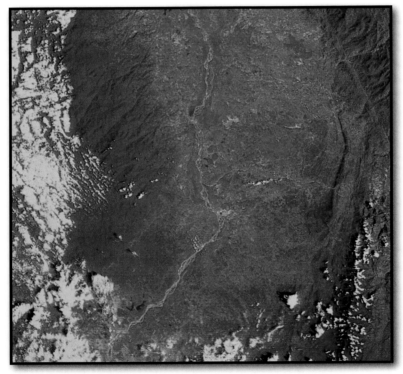

Image of a portion of the Magdalena River valley in Colombia, transmitted by Landsat (formerly ERTS) 2 on Jan. 7, 1977. Green, red, and infrared are recorded separately by the satellite and then combined to make the image. Vegetation appears red, and barren land is green. The Magdalena River and nearby lakes are blue; white splotches are clouds. The roughly parallel north-south pattern along the centre right indicates rock outcrops where the rocks have been bent into a folded structure. Courtesy of the Earth Resources Observation Systems (EROS) Data Center

shows the effects of phenomena that produce temperature variations, such as groundwater movement.

Landsat images are among the most commonly used. They are produced with data obtained from a multispectral scanner carried aboard certain U.S. Landsat satellites orbiting Earth at an altitude of about 900 km (560 miles). Images covering an area of 185 × 185 km (about 13,200 square miles) are available for every segment of Earth's surface. Scanner measurements are made in four spectral bands: green and red in the visible portion of the spectrum, and two infrared bands. The data are usually displayed by arbitrarily assigning different colours to the bands and then superimposing these to make "false-colour" images.

In geology, Landsat images are used to delineate landforms, rock outcrops and surface lithology, structural features, hydrothermal areas, and sites of mineral resources. Changes in vegetation revealed in the images may distinguish different soil types, subtle elevation differences, subsurface water distribution, subcropping rocks, and trace element distribution, among other things.

LANDSAT

Landsat, which is the byname of Earth Resources Technology Satellite (ERTS), is the name for any of a series of unmanned U.S. scientific satellites. The first three Landsat satellites were launched in 1972, 1975, and 1978. These satellites were primarily designed to collect information about Earth's natural resources, including the location of mineral deposits and the condition of forests and farming regions. They were also equipped to monitor atmospheric and oceanic conditions and to detect variations in pollution level and other ecological changes. All three satellites carried various types of cameras, including those with infrared sensors. Landsat cameras provided images of surface areas

115 miles (184 km) square; each such area could be photographed at 18-day intervals. These pictures were the basis of a far more comprehensive survey than could be made from airplanes.

A fourth Landsat satellite was launched in 1982 and a fifth in 1984. In 1985 Landsat was transferred to a private commercial operator, the Earth Observation Satellite Company (EOSAT). In 1992 the U.S. government again assumed control of the program. The newer models contained two sensors, a multispectral scanner and a thematic mapper (which provides 100-foot [30-metre] spatial resolution in seven spectral bands). Landsat 6 failed to achieve orbit after its launch in 1993. Landsat 7 was launched successfully in 1999. Because Landsat 5 and 7 are nearing the end of their operational lifetimes, a new satellite, the Landsat Data Continuity Mission, is planned for launch in December 2012.

Lineations of features may distinguish folded-rock strata or fault ruptures even where the primary features are not evident.

Magnetic Methods

Measurements can be made of Earth's total magnetic field or of components of the field in various directions. The oldest magnetic prospecting instrument is the magnetic compass, which measures the field direction. Other instruments include magnetic balances and fluxgate magnetometers. Most magnetic surveys are made with proton-precession or optical-pumping magnetometers, which are appreciably more accurate. The proton magnetometer measures a radio-frequency voltage induced in a coil by the reorientation (precession) of magnetically polarized protons in a container of ordinary water. The optical-pumping magnetometer makes use of the principles of nuclear resonance and cesium or rubidium vapour.

It can detect minute magnetic fluctuations by measuring the effects of light-induced (optically pumped) transitions between atomic energy levels that are dependent on magnetic field strength.

Magnetic surveys are usually made with magnetometers borne by aircraft flying in parallel lines spaced 2 to 4 km (about 1.2 to 2.5 miles) apart at an elevation of about 500 metres (1,640 feet) when exploring for petroleum deposits and in lines 0.5 to 1 km (0.3 to 0.6 mile) apart roughly 200 metres (about 660 feet) above the ground when searching for mineral concentrations. Ground surveys are conducted to follow up magnetic anomaly discoveries made from the air. Such surveys may involve stations spaced only 50 metres (about 165 feet) apart. Magnetometers also are towed by research vessels. In some cases, two or more magnetometers displaced a few metres from each other are used in a gradiometer arrangement; differences between their readings indicate the magnetic field gradient. A ground monitor is usually used to measure the natural fluctuations of Earth's field over time so that corrections can be made. Surveying is generally suspended during periods of large magnetic fluctuation (magnetic storms).

Magnetic effects result primarily from the magnetization induced in susceptible rocks by Earth's magnetic field. Most sedimentary rocks have very low susceptibility and thus are nearly transparent to magnetism. Accordingly, in petroleum exploration magnetics are used negatively: magnetic anomalies indicate the absence of explorable sedimentary rocks. Magnetics are used for mapping features in igneous and metamorphic rocks, possibly faults, dikes, or other features that are associated with mineral concentrations. Data are usually displayed in the form of a contour map of the magnetic field, but interpretation is often made on profiles.

MAGNETOMETER

A magnetometer is an instrument for measuring the strength and sometimes the direction of magnetic fields, including those on or near Earth and in space. Magnetometers are also used to calibrate electromagnets and permanent magnets, and to determine the magnetization of materials.

Magnetometers specifically used to measure Earth's field are of two types, absolute and relative, which are classed by their methods of calibration. Absolute magnetometers are calibrated with reference to their own known internal constants. Relative magnetometers must be calibrated by reference to a known, accurately measured magnetic field.

The simplest absolute magnetometer, devised by C.F. Gauss in 1832, consists of a permanent bar magnet suspended horizontally by a gold fibre. Measuring the period of oscillation of the magnet in Earth's magnetic field gives a measure of the field's strength. A widely used modern absolute instrument is the proton-precession magnetometer. It measures a voltage induced in a coil by the reorientation (precession) of magnetically polarized protons in ordinary water.

The Schmidt vertical-field balance, a relative magnetometer used in geophysical exploration, uses a horizontally balanced bar magnet equipped with mirror and knife edges.

Rocks cannot retain magnetism when the temperature is above the Curie point (about 500 °C [about 930 °F] for most magnetic materials), and this restricts magnetic rocks to the upper 40 km (25 miles) of Earth's interior. The source of the geomagnetic field must be deeper than this, and it is now believed that convection currents of conducting material in the outer core generate the field. These currents couple to Earth's spin, so that the magnetic field—when averaged over time—is oriented along the planet's axis. The currents gradually change with time in a somewhat erratic manner and their aggregate effect sometimes reverses, which explains the time changes in Earth's field. This is the crux of the magnetohydrodynamic theory of the geomagnetic field.

GRAVITY METHODS

Earth's gravity field can be measured by timing the free fall of an object in a vacuum, by measuring the period of a pendulum, or in various other ways. Today almost all gravity surveying is done with gravimeters. Such an instrument typically consists of a weight attached to a spring that stretches or contracts corresponding to an increase or decrease in gravity. It is designed to measure differences in gravity accelerations rather than absolute magnitudes. Gravimeters used in geophysical surveys have an accuracy of about 0.01 milligal (mgal; 1 mgal = 0.001 centimetre per second per second). That is to say, they are capable of detecting differences in Earth's gravitational field as small as one part in 100 million.

Gravity differences occur because of local density differences. Anomalies of exploration interest are often about 0.2 mgal. Data have to be corrected for variations due to elevation (one metre is equivalent to about 0.2 mgal), latitude (100 metres are equivalent to about 0.08 mgal), and other factors. Gravity surveys on land often involve meter readings every kilometre along traverse loops a few kilometres across. It takes only a few minutes to read a gravimeter, but determining location and elevation accurately requires much effort. Inertial navigation is sometimes used for determining elevation and location when helicopters are employed to transport gravimeters. Marine gravimeters are mounted on inertial platforms when used on surface vessels. A ship's speed and direction affect gravimeter readings and limit survey accuracy. Aircraft undergo too many accelerations to permit gravity measurements except for regional studies.

In most cases, the density of sedimentary rocks increases with depth because the increased pressure results in a loss of porosity. Uplifts usually bring denser rocks nearer the surface and thereby create positive gravity anomalies. Faults that displace rocks of different densities also can cause gravity anomalies. Salt domes generally produce negative anomalies because salt is less dense than the surrounding rocks. Such folds, faults, and salt domes trap oil, and so the detection of gravity anomalies associated with them is crucial in petroleum exploration. Moreover, gravity measurements are occasionally used to evaluate the amount of high-density mineral present in an ore body. They also provide a means of locating hidden caverns, old mine workings, and other subterranean cavities.

SEISMIC REFRACTION METHODS

Seismic methods are based on measurements of the time interval between initiation of a seismic (elastic) wave and its arrival at detectors. The seismic wave may be generated by an explosion, a dropped weight, a mechanical vibrator, a bubble of high-pressure air injected into water, or other sources. The seismic wave is detected by a Geophone on land or by a hydrophone in water. An electromagnetic Geophone generates a voltage when a seismic wave produces relative motion of a wire coil in the field of a magnet, whereas a ceramic hydrophone generates a voltage when deformed by passage of a seismic wave. Data are usually recorded on magnetic tape for subsequent processing and display.

Seismic energy travels from source to detector by many paths. When near the source, the initial seismic energy generally travels by the shortest path, but as source–Geophone distances become greater, seismic waves travelling by longer paths through rocks of higher seismic velocity may arrive earlier. Such waves are called head waves, and the refraction method involves their interpretation. From a plot of travel time as a function of source–Geophone distance, the number, thicknesses, and velocities of rock layers present can be determined for simple situations. The assumptions usually made are that (1) each layer is homogeneous and isotropic (i.e., has the same velocity in all directions); (2) the boundaries (interfaces) between layers are nearly planar; and (3) each successive layer has higher velocity than the one above. The velocity values determined from time–distance plots depend also on the dip (slope) of interfaces, apparent velocities increasing when the Geophones are updip from the source and decreasing when downdip. By measuring in both directions the dip and rock velocity, each can be determined. With sufficient measurements, relief on the interfaces separating the layers also can be ascertained.

High-velocity bodies of local extent can be located by fan shooting. Travel times are measured along different azimuths from a source, and an abnormally early arrival time indicates that a high-velocity body was encountered at that azimuth. This method has been used to detect salt domes, reefs, and intrusive bodies that are characterized by higher seismic velocity than the surrounding rock.

Two types of seismic waves can travel through a body: *P* waves (primary) and *S* waves (secondary). *P* waves are compressional waves and travel at the highest velocity; hence, they arrive first. *S* waves are shear waves that travel at a slower rate and are not able to pass through liquids that do not possess shear strength. In addition, there are several types of seismic waves that can travel along surfaces. A major type of surface wave is the Rayleigh wave,

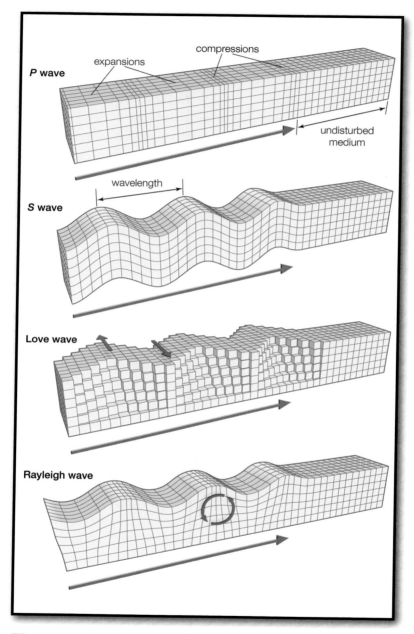

The main types of seismic waves: P, S, *Love, and Rayleigh.* Encyclopædia Britannica, Inc.

in which a particle moves in an elliptical path in the vertical plane from the source. The horizontal component of Rayleigh waves is probably the principal cause of damage from earthquakes. Another type of surface waves, Love waves, involve shear motion. Still other varieties of surface waves can be transmitted through low-velocity layers (channel waves) or along the surface of a borehole (tube waves). Under certain circumstances (e.g., oblique incidence on an interface), waves can change from one mode to another.

Most of the current knowledge about Earth's internal constitution is derived from analysis of the time–distance curves from earthquakes. Earthquakes usually generate several wave modes. These refract and reflect at interfaces within Earth and partially change to other wave types to add to the number of seismic waves resulting from an earthquake. Different wave types can sometimes be distinguished by their components of motion detected by three-component seismographs; the direction from which they come can be determined by using an array of seismographs at the receiving station or by combining the data from different stations. The first wave motion from an earthquake reveals the nature of earth motion involved in the earthquake.

Very shallow seismic refraction is extensively used in engineering studies. Sometimes the energy source for shallow-penetration engineering studies involves simply hitting the ground with a sledgehammer. The ease with which a rock can be ripped by a bulldozer relates to the rock's seismic velocity. S-wave velocity measurements are of special interest to engineers because building stability depends on the shear strength of the foundation rock or soil. Seismic waves may be used for various other purposes. They are employed, for example, to detect faults that may

SEISMIC WAVE

A seismic wave is a vibration generated by an earthquake, explosion, or similar energetic source and propagated within Earth or along its surface. Earthquakes generate four principal types of elastic waves; two, known as body waves, travel within Earth, whereas the other two, called surface waves, travel along its surface. Seismographs record the amplitude and frequency of seismic waves and yield information about Earth and its subsurface structure. Artificially generated seismic waves recorded during seismic surveys are used to collect data in oil and gas prospecting and engineering.

P waves, also called compressional or longitudinal waves, give the transmitting medium—whether liquid, solid, or gas—a back-and-forth motion in the direction of the path of propagation, thus stretching or compressing the medium as the wave passes any one point in a manner similar to that of sound waves in air. Within Earth, *P* waves travel at speeds from about 6 km (3.7 miles) per second in surface rock to about 10.4 km (6.5 miles) per second near Earth's core some 2,900 km (1,800 miles) below the surface. As the waves enter the core, the velocity drops to about 8 km (5 miles) per second. It increases to about 11 km (6.8 miles) per second near Earth's centre. The speed increase with depth results from increased hydrostatic pressure as well as from changes in rock composition. In general, the increase causes *P* waves to travel in curved paths that are concave upward.

S waves, also called shear or transverse waves, cause points of solid media to move back and forth perpendicular to the direction of propagation; as the wave passes, the medium is sheared first in one direction and then in another. Within Earth the speed of *S* waves increases from about 3.4 km (2.1 miles) per second at the surface to 7.2 km (4.5 miles) per second near the boundary of the core, which, being liquid, cannot transmit them; indeed, their observed absence is a compelling argument for the liquid nature of the outer core. Like *P* waves, *S* waves travel in curved paths that are concave upward.

Of the two surface seismic waves, Love waves—named after the British seismologist A.E.H. Love, who first predicted their existence—travel faster. They are propagated when the solid medium near the surface has varying vertical elastic properties. Displacement of the medium by the wave is entirely perpendicular to the direction of propagation and has no vertical or longitudinal components. The energy of Love waves, like that of other surface waves, spreads from the source in two directions rather than in three, and so these waves produce a strong record at seismic stations even when originating from distant earthquakes.

The other principal surface waves are called Rayleigh waves after the British physicist Lord Rayleigh, who first mathematically demonstrated their existence. Rayleigh waves travel along the free surface of an elastic solid such as Earth. Their motion is a combination of longitudinal compression and dilation that results in an elliptical motion of points on the surface. Of all seismic waves, Rayleigh waves spread out most in time, producing a long wave duration on seismographs.

disrupt a coal seam or fractures that may allow water penetration into a tunnel.

SEISMIC REFLECTION METHODS

Most seismic work utilizes reflection techniques. Sources and Geophones are essentially the same as those used in refraction methods. The concept is similar to echo sounding: seismic waves are reflected at interfaces where rock properties change and the round-trip travel time, together with velocity information, gives the distance to the interface. The relief on the interface can be determined by mapping the reflection at many locations. For simple situations the velocity can be determined from the change in arrival time as source–Geophone distance changes.

In practice, the seismic reflection method is much more complicated. Reflections from most of the many interfaces within Earth are very weak and so do not stand out against background noise. The reflections from closely spaced interfaces interfere with each other. Reflections from interfaces with different dips, seismic waves that bounce repeatedly between interfaces ("multiples"), converted waves, and waves travelling by other modes interfere with desired reflections. Also, velocity irregularities bend seismic rays in ways that are sometimes complicated.

The objective of most seismic work is to map geologic structure by determining the arrival time of reflectors. Changes in the amplitude and waveshape, however, contain information about stratigraphic changes and occasionally hydrocarbon accumulations. In some cases, seismic patterns can be identified with depositional systems, unconformities, channels, and other features.

The seismic reflection method usually gives better resolution (i.e., makes it possible to see smaller features) than other methods, with the exception of measurements made in close proximity, as with borehole logs. Appreciably more funds are expended on seismic reflection work than on all other geophysical methods combined.

ELECTRICAL AND ELECTROMAGNETIC METHODS

A multitude of electrical methods are used in mineral exploration. They depend on electrochemical activity, resistivity changes, or permittivity effects. Some materials tend to become natural batteries that generate natural electric currents whose effects can be measured. The self-potential method relies on the oxidation of the upper surface of metallic sulfide minerals by downward-percolating groundwater to become a natural battery; current flows through the ore body and back through the surrounding groundwater, which acts as the electrolyte. Measuring the natural voltage differences (usually 50–400 millivolts [mV]) permits detecting continuous metallic sulfide bodies that lie astride the water table. Graphite, magnetite, anthracite, some pyritized rocks, and other phenomena also can generate self-potentials.

The passage of an electric current across an interface where conduction changes from ionic to electronic results in a charge buildup at the interface. This charge builds up shortly after current flow begins, and it takes a short time to decay after the current circuit is broken. Such an effect is measured in induced-polarization methods and is used to detect sulfide ore bodies.

Resistivity methods involve passing a current from a generator or other electric power source between a pair of current electrodes and measuring potential differences with another pair of electrodes. Various electrode configurations are used to determine the apparent resistivity from the voltage/current ratio. The resistivity of most rocks varies with porosity, the salinity of the interstitial fluid, and certain other factors. Rocks containing appreciable clay usually have low resistivity. The resistivity of rocks containing conducting minerals such as sulfide ores and graphitized or pyritized rocks depends on the connectivity of the minerals present. Resistivity methods also are used in engineering and groundwater surveys, because resistivity often changes markedly at soil/bedrock interfaces, at the water table, and at a fresh/saline water boundary.

Investigators can determine how resistivity varies over a given area by means of profiling methods, in which the location of an array of electrodes is altered but the same spacing between the component electrodes is maintained. Sounding methods enable investigators to pinpoint variations of resistivity with depth. In this case, electrode spacing is increased and, correspondingly, the effective depth of the contributing section. Several other techniques are commonly employed. Equipotential methods entail mapping equipotential lines that result from a current. Distortions from a systematic pattern indicate the presence of a body of different resistivity. The mise-a-la-masse method involves putting one current electrode in an ore body in order to map its shape and location.

The passage of current in the general frequency range of 500–5,000 hertz (Hz) induces in Earth electromagnetic waves of long wavelength, which have considerable penetration into Earth's interior. The effective penetration can be changed by altering the frequency. Eddy currents are induced where conductors are present, and these currents generate an alternating magnetic field, which induces in a receiving coil a secondary voltage that is out of phase with the primary voltage. Electromagnetic methods involve measuring this out-of-phase component or other effects, which makes it possible to locate low-resistivity ore bodies wherein the eddy currents are generated.

Natural currents are induced in Earth as a result of atmospheric disturbances (e.g., lightning strikes) and bombardment of the upper atmosphere by the solar wind—a radial flow of protons, electrons, and nuclei of heavier elements emanating from the outer region of the Sun. Magnetotelluric methods measure orthogonal components of the electric and magnetic fields induced by these natural currents. Such measurements allow researchers to determine resistivity as a function of depth. The natural currents span a broad range of frequencies and thus a range of effective penetration depths. Related to the above techniques is the telluric-current method, in which the electric current variations are measured simultaneously at two stations. Comparison of the data permits determining differences in the apparent resistivity with depth at the two stations.

Electrical methods generally do not penetrate far into Earth, and so do not yield much information about its deeper parts. They do, however, provide a valuable tool of exploring for many metal ores.

In addition, several electrical methods are used in boreholes. The self-potential (SP) log indicates mainly clay (shale) content, because an electrochemical cell is established at the shale boundary when the salinity of the borehole (drilling) fluid differs from that of the water in the rock. Resistivity measurements are made by using several electrode configurations and also by induction. Borehole methods are used to identify the rocks penetrated by a borehole and to determine their properties, especially their porosity and the nature of their interstitial fluids.

RADIOACTIVE METHODS

Radioactive surveys are used to detect ores or rock bodies associated with radioactive materials. Most natural radioactivity derives from uranium, thorium, and a radioisotope of potassium (potassium-40), as well as from radon gas. Radioactive elements are concentrated chiefly in the upper portion of Earth's crust.

Radioactive disintegration, or decay, gives rise to spontaneous emission of alpha and beta particles and gamma rays. Detection is usually of gamma rays, and it is accomplished in most cases with a scintillometer, a photoconversion device containing a crystal of sodium iodide that emits a photon (minute packet of electromagnetic radiation) when struck by a gamma ray. The photon, whose intensity is proportional to the energy of the gamma ray, causes an adjacent photocathode to emit electrons, the exact number depending on the energy of the photon. The energy of the gamma ray itself is determined by the nature of the radioactive disintegration involved.

Where it can be assumed that a product element of a radioactive disintegration (a daughter isotope) is derived solely from the disintegration of a parent isotope that occurred after a rock's solidification (i.e., as the rock cooled through its Curie point), the ratio of the parent/daughter isotopes present depends on the time since solidification. This often provides the basis for age determinations of rocks.

Information about the mineral composition and physical properties of a rock formation can be obtained by means of gamma-ray logging, a technique that involves measuring natural gamma-ray emissions in boreholes. In most sedimentary rocks, for example, potassium-40 is the principal emitter of gamma rays. Because potassium is generally associated with clays, a recording of gamma-ray emissions permits determination of clay (shale) content. In another related technique, the rock surrounding a borehole is bombarded by a radioactive source in the logging sonde and the effects of the reactions caused by the bombardment are measured. In a density log measurements are made of gamma rays that are backscattered from the rock formation, since their intensity indicates rock density. A neutron source is employed in another type of borehole log, one that is designed to reveal how much fluid occurs in a rock formation or how porous it is. Neutron energy loss is directly related to the density of protons (hydrogen nuclei) in rock, which is in turn reflective of its water content (or degree of porosity). These borehole logging techniques are used often in the oil and natural gas industries to assist in the exploration and determination of reservoirs.

Geothermal Methods

Temperature-gradient measurements are sometimes made to detect heat-flow anomalies. However, most exploration for geothermal resources (e.g., superheated water and steam) is done via indirect methods. Resistivity or seismic methods, for example, may be used to map the magma chamber, which is the source of the heat, or to detect faults or other features that control the flow of hot subsurface water.

GEOCHEMICAL METHODS

Since the early 1970s researchers have developed extremely sensitive methods of chemical analysis, providing the ability to detect minute amounts of materials. Many chemical elements are transported in very small quantities by fluids flowing in Earth, so that a systematic measurement of such trace elements may help in locating their sources. Trace elements are sometimes associated with hydrocarbons (the principal constituents of petroleum, natural gas, and other fossil fuels); they can be utilized for identifying the specific types of hydrocarbons present in a given area. Geochemical soil maps of small areas or whole countries are used to locate industrial wastes, areas of soil contamination, and sites of pollution discharge to rivers.

EXCAVATION, BORING, AND SAMPLING

Direct sampling, usually by means of boreholes, is required to make positive identification of ores, fuels, and other materials. It is also necessary for determining their quantity and for selecting methods of recovery.

Most deep boreholes are drilled by the rotary method, in which a drill bit is rotated while fluid ("drilling mud") is circulated through the bit to lubricate and cool it and to bring rock chips to the surface where they can be collected and analyzed. Shallow boreholes in hard rock formations are sometimes drilled by a percussion method, whereby a heavy bit is repeatedly raised and dropped to chip away

Preparing to drill a borehole using a large, rotating bit. Shutterstock.com

pieces of rock. After a borehole has been drilled, various tools—sondes—are lowered into the hole to measure different physical properties.

DEEP EARTH

The overall oblate shape of Earth was established by French Academy expeditions between 1735 and 1743. Earth's mean density and total mass were determined by the English physicist and chemist Henry Cavendish in about 1797. It was later ascertained that the density of rocks on Earth's surface is significantly less than the mean density, leading to the assumption that the density of the deeper parts of the planet must be much greater.

Earth's magnetic field was first studied by William Gilbert of England during the late 1500s. Since that time a long sequence of measurements has indicated its overall dipole nature, with ample evidence that it is more complex than the field of a simple dipole. Investigators also have demonstrated that the geomagnetic field changes over time. Moreover, they have found that magnetic constituents within rocks take on magnetic orientations as the rocks cool through their Curie point or, in the case of sedimentary rocks, as they are deposited. A rock tends to retain its magnetic orientation, so that measuring it provides information about Earth's magnetic field at the time of the rock's formation and how the rock has moved since then. The field of study specifically concerned with this subject is called paleomagnetism.

Observations of earthquake waves by the mid-1900s had led to a spherically symmetrical crust–mantle–core picture of Earth. The crust–mantle boundary is marked by a fairly large increase in velocity at the Mohorovičić discontinuity at depths on the order of 25–40 km (16–25 miles) on the continents and 5–8 km (3–5 miles) on the seafloor. The mantle–core boundary is the Gutenberg discontinuity at a depth of about 2,800 km (1,740 miles). The outer core is thought to be liquid because shear waves do not pass through it.

Scientific understanding of Earth began undergoing a revolution from the 1950s. Theories of continental drift and seafloor spreading evolved into plate tectonics, the concept that the upper, primarily rigid part of Earth, the lithosphere, is floating on a plastic asthenosphere and that the lithosphere is being moved by slow convection currents in the upper mantle. The plates spread from the mid-oceanic ridges where new oceanic crust is being formed, and they are destroyed by plunging back into the asthenosphere at subduction zones where they collide. Lithospheric plates also may slide past one another along strike-slip or transform faults. Most earthquakes occur at the subduction zones or along strike-slip faults, but some minor ones occur in rift zones. The apparent fit of the bulge of eastern South America into the bight of Africa, magnetic stripes on the ocean floors, earthquake distribution, paleomagnetic data, and various other observations are now regarded as natural consequences of a single plate-tectonics model. The model has many applications. It explains much inferred Earth history and suggests where hydrocarbons and minerals are most likely to be found. Its acceptance has been widespread as economic conclusions have borne fruit.

An extensive series of boreholes drilled into the seafloor under the Joint Oceanographic Institutions for Deep Earth Sampling (JOIDES) program has established a relatively simple picture of the crust beneath the oceans. In the rift zones where the plates comprising Earth's thin crust separate, material from the mantle wells upward, cools, and solidifies. The molten mantle material that flows onto the seafloor and cools rapidly is called pillow basalt, while the underlying material that cools more slowly forms gabbros and sheeted dikes. Sediments gradually accumulate on top of these, producing a comparatively simple pattern of sediment, basaltic basement, gabbroic layering, and underlying mantle structure. Much of the heat flow from the solid Earth into the oceans results from the slow cooling of the oceanic rocks. Heat flow gradually declines with distance from the spreading centres (or with the length of time since solidification). As the oceanic rocks cool they become slightly denser, and isostatic adjustment causes them to subside slightly so that oceanic depths become greater.

The oceanic crust is relatively thin, measuring only about 5–8 km (3–5 miles) in thickness. Nearly all oceanic rocks are fairly young, mostly Jurassic or younger (i.e., less than 200 million years old), but relics of ocean floor rocks have been found in ophiolite complexes as old as 3.8 billion years.

The crust within the continents, unlike the oceanic crust, is considerably older and thicker and appears to have been formed in a much more complex way. Because of its greater thickness, diversity, and complexity, the continental crust is much more difficult to explore. In 1975 the U.S. Geodynamics Committee initiated a research program to explore the continental crust using seismic techniques developed by private industry for the purpose of locating petroleum accumulations in sedimentary rocks. Since then its investigations have been conducted in a number of locales throughout the United States. Several notable findings have resulted from these studies, the most spectacular of which was the discovery of a succession of very low-angle thrust sheets beneath the Appalachian Mountains. This discovery, made from seismic reflection profiling data, influenced later theories on continent formation.

A Texas A&M scientist examines seafloor samples collected as part of the Joint Oceanographic Institutions for Deep Earth Sampling (JOIDES) program. © AP Images

The success of the U.S. crustal studies program has spawned a series of similar efforts in Australia, Canada, Europe, India, the Tibet Autonomous Region of China, and elsewhere, and seismic investigation of the continental crust continues to be one of the most active areas of basic exploration.

The desire to detect nuclear explosions in the years following World War II led to the establishment of a worldwide network of uniform seismograph stations. This has greatly increased the number and reliability of earthquake measurements, the major source of information about Earth's interior. The construction of large-array seismograph stations has made it possible to determine the directions of approach of earthquake waves and to sort out overlapping wave trains. Computer processing allows investigators to separate many wave effects from background noise and to analyze the implications of the multitude of observations now available.

The assumptions made in the past that significant property variations occur mainly in the vertical direction were clearly an oversimplification. Today, investigation of the deep Earth concentrates primarily on determining lateral (horizontal) changes and on interpreting their significance. Seismic tomographic analysis records variations in the seismic velocity of Earth's subsurface and has revolutionized the imaging and definition of mantle plumes (hot material originating from the core-mantle boundary) and subducting lithospheric plates.

CONCLUSION

The development of the geologic sciences has played out over many centuries. From the earliest formal investigations of minerals by the Greek philosopher and naturalist

Theophrastus to the deep Earth investigations of the present day, work in the geological sciences has contributed much to the greater scientific understanding of planet Earth and the universe in which it resides.

The quest to learn about Earth's surface and subsurface has been strengthened over the years by the development of new technologies and instrumentation, as well as by the perspectives offered by great thinkers such as James Charles Lyell (uniformitarianism) and Alfred Wegener (continental drift). These and discoveries made by others, such as Nicolaus Steno (fossils) and Robert Sinclair Dietz, Drummond Matthews, and Frederick Vine (plate tectonics), precipitated revolutions in thought that led to the modern understanding of geology and its subdisciplines.

Although much has been learned to date, humans will continue to plumb Earth's depths with increasingly sophisticated technology. Future discoveries will either support existing ideas about Earth's formation and development or overturn them in favour of new paradigms.

CHAPTER 4
NOTABLE EARTH SCIENTISTS

The modern scientific understanding of the geological sciences rests upon the contributions made by scientists throughout history. The lives and contributions of some of the more influential Earth scientists—including James Hutton, Charles Lyell, Jöns Jacob Berzelius, Louis Agassiz, and William Thompson (Baron Kelvin)—are presented herein, in alphabetical order.

(JEAN) LOUIS (RODOLPHE) AGASSIZ

(b. May 28, 1807, Motier, Switz.—d. Dec. 14, 1873, Cambridge, Mass., U.S.)

Louis Agassiz was a Swiss-born U.S. naturalist, geologist, and teacher who made revolutionary contributions to the study of natural science with landmark work on glacier activity and extinct fishes. He achieved lasting fame through his innovative teaching methods, which altered the character of natural science education in the United States.

EARLY LIFE

Agassiz was the son of the Protestant pastor of Motier, a village on the shore of Lake Morat, Switz. In boyhood he attended the gymnasium in Bienne and later the academy at Lausanne. He entered the universities of Zürich,

Heidelberg, and Munich and took at Erlangen the degree of doctor of philosophy and at Munich that of doctor of medicine.

As a youth he gave some attention to the ways of the brook fish of western Switzerland, but his permanent interest in ichthyology began with his study of an extensive collection of Brazilian fishes, mostly from the Amazon River, which had been collected in 1819 and 1820 by two eminent naturalists at Munich. The classification of these species was begun by one of the collectors in 1826, and when he died the collection was turned over to Agassiz. The work was completed and published in 1829 as *Selecta Genera et Species Piscium.* The study of fish forms became henceforth the prominent feature of his research. In 1830 he issued a prospectus of a *History of the Fresh Water Fishes of Central Europe,* printed in parts from 1839 to 1842.

The year 1832 proved the most significant in Agassiz's early career because it took him first to Paris, then the centre of scientific research, and later to Neuchâtel, Switz., where he spent many years of fruitful effort. While in Paris he lived the life of an impecunious student in the Latin Quarter, supporting himself and helped at times by the kindly interest of such friends as the German naturalist Alexander von Humboldt—who secured for him a professorship at Neuchâtel—and Baron Cuvier, the most eminent ichthyologist of his time.

Already Agassiz had become interested in the rich stores of the extinct fishes of Europe, especially those of Glarus in Switzerland and of Monte Bolca near Verona, of which, at that time, only a few had been critically studied. As early as 1829 Agassiz planned a comprehensive and critical study of these fossils and spent much time gathering material wherever possible. His epoch-making work, *Recherches sur les poissons fossiles,* appeared in parts from 1833 to 1843. In it, the number of named fossil fishes was raised to more than 1,700, and the ancient seas were made to live again through the descriptions of their inhabitants. The great importance of this fundamental work rests on the impetus it gave to the study of extinct life itself. Turning his attention to other extinct animals found with the fishes, Agassiz published in 1838–42 two volumes on the fossil echinoderms of Switzerland, and later (1841–42) his *Études critiques sur les mollusques fossiles*.

From 1832 to 1846 he served as professor of natural history in the University of Neuchâtel. In Neuchâtel he acted for a time as his own publisher, and his private residence became a hive of activity with numerous young men assisting him. He now began his *Nomenclator Zoologicus,* a catalog with references of all the names applied to genera of animals from the beginning of scientific nomenclature, a date since fixed at Jan. 1, 1758.

In 1836 Agassiz began a new line of studies: the movements and effects of the glaciers of Switzerland. Several writers had expressed the opinion that these rivers of ice once had been much more extensive and that the erratic boulders scattered over the region and up to the summit of the Jura Mountains were carried by moving glaciers. On the ice of the Aar Glacier he built a hut, the "Hôtel des Neuchâtelois," from which he and his associates traced

Louis Agassiz, undated engraving. Photos.com/Jupiterimages

the structure and movements of the ice. In 1840 he published his *Études sur les glaciers,* in some respects his most important work. In it, Agassiz showed that at a geologically recent period Switzerland had been covered by one vast ice sheet. His final conclusion was that "great sheets of ice, resembling those now existing in Greenland, once covered all the countries in which unstratified gravel (boulder drift) is found."

ACTIVITIES IN THE UNITED STATES

In 1846 Agassiz visited the United States for the general purpose of studying natural history and geology there but more specifically to give a course of lectures at the Lowell Institute in Boston. The lectures were followed by another series in Charleston and, later, by both popular and technical lectures in various cities. In 1847 he accepted a professorship of zoology at Harvard University. In 1850, after his first wife's death, he married Elizabeth Cabot Cary of Boston, who was well known as a writer and a promoter of women's education.

In the United States his chief volumes of scientific research were the following: *Lake Superior* (1850); *Contributions to the Natural History of the United States* (1857–62), in four quarto volumes, the most notable being on the embryology of turtles; and the *Essay on Classification* (1859), a brilliant publication, which, however, failed to grasp the fact that zoology was moving away from the doctrine of special creation toward the doctrine of evolution. Besides these extensive contributions there appeared a multitude of short papers on natural history and especially on the fishes of the United States. His two expeditions of most importance were, first, to Brazil in 1865 and, second, to California in 1871, the latter trip involving both shores of South America. *A Journey in Brazil* (1868), written by Mrs. Agassiz and himself, gives an account of their experiences. His most important paper on U.S. fishes dealt with the group of viviparous surf fishes of California.

Agassiz was deeply absorbed in his cherished plan of developing at Harvard a comprehensive museum of zoological research. This institution, which was established in 1859 and ultimately grew into the present museum of comparative zoology, enjoyed his fostering care during the rest of his lifetime. In the United States, Agassiz's industry and devotion to scientific pursuits continued, but two other traits now assumed importance. Quite possibly he was the ablest science teacher, administrator, promoter, and fundraiser in the United States in the 19th century. In addition, he was devoted to his students, who were in the highest sense coworkers with him.

Agassiz's method as teacher was to give contact with nature rather than information. He discouraged the use of books except in detailed research. The result of his instruction at Harvard was a complete revolution in the study of natural history in the United States. The purpose of study was not to acquire a category of facts from others but to be able, through active contact with the natural world, to gather the needed facts. As a result of his activities, every notable teacher of natural history in the United States for the second half of the 19th century was a pupil either of Agassiz or of one of his students.

In the interests of better teaching and of scientific enthusiasm, he organized in the summer of 1873 the Anderson School of Natural History at Penikese, an island in Buzzards Bay. This school, which had the greatest influence on science teaching in America, was run solely by Agassiz. After his death it vanished.

AGASSIZ AND DARWIN

Because Agassiz was beyond question one of the ablest, wisest, and best informed of the biologists of his day, it may be asked why his attitude toward Darwin's *Origin of Species,* published in 1859, was cold and unsympathetic. It is likely that Agassiz's lifelong view of nature determined his attitude toward the new doctrine of evolution. Although Agassiz was quite familiar with the factual evidence concerning environmental change, variability, and hereditary modification on which Darwin built his arguments, he held that the organic world represented repeated interventions by the Supreme Being. Ordinary physical events on which Darwin relied, such as climatic and geologic change, and even glaciers, could bring about extinctions but not new species. The sequence in the fossil record from simple animals and plants in the ancient, deeper strata to the more complex, recent forms found near the surface represented a progressive development, Agassiz agreed, but these different animals and plants did not arise because of interactions between populations and external environmental changes, as Darwin argued. Agassiz maintained that since organisms arose by a series of independent and special creations, there could be no hereditary continuity between different types of organisms. Each species of plant and animal was a "thought of God," and homologies or anatomical similarities were "associations of ideas in the Divine Mind." Agassiz's view of nature was historically derived from the thought of Plato, for whom the unseen world had more reality than the world of sense experience. Agassiz, therefore, could not accept Darwin's conceptual view of nature, in which environmental events could evoke organic change.

GEORGIUS AGRICOLA

(b. March 24, 1494, Clauchau, Sax.—d. Nov. 21, 1555, Chem.)

Georgius Agricola (German: Georg Bauer) was a German scholar and scientist known as "the father of mineralogy." While a highly educated classicist and humanist, well regarded by scholars of his own and later times, he was yet singularly independent of the theories of ancient authorities. He was indeed among the first to found a natural science upon observation, as opposed to speculation. His *De re metallica* dealt chiefly with the arts of mining and smelting. His *De natura fossilium*, considered the first mineralogy textbook, presented the first scientific classification of minerals (based on their physical properties) and described many new minerals, their occurrence, and mutual relationships.

LIFE

Agricola was born of obscure parentage. From 1514 to 1518 he studied classics, philosophy, and philology at the University of Leipzig, which had recently been exposed to the humanist revival. Following the custom of the times, he Latinized his name to Georgius Agricola. After teaching Latin and Greek from 1518 to 1522 in a school in Zwickau, he returned to Leipzig to begin the study of medicine but found the university in disarray because of theological quarrels. A lifelong Catholic, he left in 1523 for more congenial surroundings in Italy. He studied medicine, natural science, and philosophy in Bologna and Padua, finishing with clinical studies in Venice.

For two years Agricola worked at the Aldine Press in Venice, principally in preparing an edition of Galen's works on medicine (published in 1525). In this task he collaborated with John Clement, who had been Thomas More's secretary during the writing of *Utopia*. More's book may well have influenced Agricola to concern himself later with the laws and social customs of the Saxon mining district. In Italy he also met and won the friendship of the great scholar Erasmus, who encouraged him to write and later published several of his books. (Erasmus wrote an introduction to Agricola's first book, the mineralogical treatise *Bermannus*. Agricola shared that honour with More and only three other scholars.)

In 1526 Agricola returned to Saxony, and from 1527 to 1533 he was town physician in Joachimsthal, a mining town in the richest metal-mining district of Europe. Partly in the hope of finding new drugs among the ores and minerals of his adopted district (a hope eventually to be disappointed), he spent all his spare time visiting mines and smelting plants, talking to the better-educated miners, and reading classical authors on mining. These years shaped the rest of his life and provided the subject matter for most of his books, beginning with *Bermannus; sive, de re metallica* (1530), a treatise on the Ore Mountains (Erzgebirge) mining district. There are indications that he owned a share in a silver mine.

Agricola appears not to have been particularly distinguished as a physician, though in this pursuit he made use of direct observation rather than of received authority. He introduced the practice of quarantine into Germany, and his books make many references to miners' occupational diseases. In 1533 he became town physician in Chemnitz, where he remained to the end of his life.

In 1546 Duke Maurice, elector of Saxony, appointed Agricola burgomaster (mayor) of Chemnitz. He also served as an emissary in the Protestant ruler Maurice's ambiguous negotiations with Charles V, the Holy Roman emperor.

The religious wars of the period rapidly eroded the tolerance that had hitherto prevailed in the Protestant German states, a tolerance from which Agricola had benefitted.

Apart from his diplomatic role, Agricola took only limited interest in politics. His youthful "Turkish Speech" of 1529, a vigorous call to the Holy Roman emperor Ferdinand I to undertake a war against the Turks, was a patriotic hymn to Germany and a call to political and religious unity. It made a great impression on the public and was often reprinted.

Chief Works

Agricola's magnum opus, for which the treatise *Bermannus* was a prelude, was *De re metallica*, published posthumously in 1556. In it, among other things, Agricola surveys historical and Classical allusions to metals and assesses the content and distribution of metal mines in antiquity. He treats the pattern of ownership and the system of law governing Saxon mines, together with the details of their day-to-day labour management. He was mainly concerned, however, with mining and metallurgy, and he discussed the geology of ore bodies, surveying, mine construction, pumping, and ventilation. There is much on the application of waterpower. He describes the assaying of ores, the methods used for enriching ores before smelting, and procedures for smelting and refining a number of metals; and he concludes with a discussion of the production of glass and of a variety of chemicals used in smelting operations.

In *De natura fossilium* (the book on which rests his right to be regarded as the father of mineralogy), Agricola offers a classification of minerals (called "fossils" at that time) in terms of geometric form (spheres, cones, plates). He was probably the first to distinguish between "simple" substances and "compounds." In Agricola's day, chemical knowledge was almost nonexistent, and there was no proper chemical analysis (other than analysis of ores by the use of fire), so the classification of ores was necessarily crude.

In several other books, notably *De natura eorum quae effluunt ex terra* (1546) and *De ortu et causis subterraneorum* (1546), Agricola describes his ideas on the origin of ore deposits in veins and correctly attributes them to deposition from aqueous solution. He also describes in detail the erosive action of rivers and its effect in the shaping of mountains. His readiness to discard received authority, even that of classical authors such as Aristotle and Pliny, is impressive.

Agricola's scholarly contemporaries regarded him highly. Erasmus prophesied in 1531 that he would "shortly stand at the head of the princes of scholarship." Later Goethe was to liken him to Francis Bacon. Melanchthon praised his "grace of presentation and unprecedented clarity." The mining engineer Herbert Hoover (later U.S. president), who translated *De re metallica* into English in 1912, regarded Agricola as the originator of the experimental approach to science, "the first to found any of the natural sciences upon research and observation, as opposed to previous fruitless speculation."

JÖNS JACOB BERZELIUS

(b. Aug. 20, 1779, near Linköping, Swed.—d. Aug. 7, 1848, Stockholm)

Jöns Jacob Berzelius was one of the founders of modern chemistry. He is especially noted for his determination of atomic weights, the development of modern chemical symbols, his electrochemical theory, the discovery and isolation of several elements, the development of classical analytical techniques, and his investigation of isomerism and catalysis, phenomena that owe their names to him. His work led to better chemical analysis in mineralogy, as well as the discovery of several new elements. He was a strict empiricist and insisted that any new theory be consistent with the sum of chemical knowledge.

EDUCATION AND CAREER

Berzelius studied medicine at Uppsala University from 1796 to 1802, and from 1807 to 1832 he served as a professor of medicine and pharmacy at the Karolinska Institute. He became a member of the Royal Swedish Academy of Sciences in 1808, serving from 1818 as its principal functionary, the perpetual secretary. In recognition of his growing international reputation, Berzelius was elevated to a position of nobility in 1818 on the coronation of King Charles XIV John. He was awarded a baronetcy in 1835 upon his marriage to Elizabeth Poppius. Together they had no children.

Berzelius was an early Swedish supporter of the new chemistry proposed a generation earlier by the renowned French chemist Antoine Lavoisier, and he remained a forceful exponent of enlightenment science and progressive politics even as romanticism pervaded Sweden and Europe. After initially aspiring to a career in physiological, especially animal, chemistry, he shifted his interests toward inorganic chemistry, the field in which he made his chief contributions. He eventually devoted considerable time to organic chemistry as well.

ELECTROCHEMICAL DUALISM

Berzelius is best known for his system of electrochemical dualism. The electrical battery, invented in 1800 by

Alessandro Volta and known as the voltaic pile, provided the first experimental source of current electricity. In 1803 Berzelius demonstrated, as did the English chemist Humphry Davy at a slightly later date, the power of the voltaic pile to decompose chemicals into pairs of electrically opposite constituents. For example, water decomposed into electropositive hydrogen and electronegative oxygen, whereas salts degraded into electronegative acids and electropositive bases. Based upon this evidence, Berzelius revised and generalized the acid/base chemistry chiefly promoted by Lavoisier. For Berzelius, all chemical compounds contained two electrically opposing constituents, the acidic, or electronegative, and the basic, or electropositive. His generalization elevated bases from their formerly passive role as mere substrates upon which acids reacted to form salts to substances having characteristic properties opposite those of acids. He also generalized about the electrochemical dualism of other substances including unusual inorganic compounds such as the chlorides of sulfur, double and higher salts, naturally occurring minerals, and organic compounds. According to Berzelius, all chemicals, whether natural or artificial, mineral or organic, could be distinguished and specified qualitatively by identifying their electrically opposing constituents.

STOICHIOMETRY

In addition to his qualitative specification of chemicals, Berzelius investigated their quantitative relationships as well. As early as 1806, he began to prepare an up-to-date Swedish chemistry textbook and read widely on the subject of chemical combination. Finding little information on the subject, he decided to undertake further investigations. His pedagogical interest focused his attention upon inorganic chemistry. Around 1808 he launched what became a vast and enduring program in the laboratory analysis of inorganic matter. To this end, he created most of his apparatuses and prepared his own reagents. Through precise experimental trials, supported by extraordinary interpretive acumen, he established the atomic weights of the elements, the formulas of their oxides, sulfides, and salts, and the formulas of virtually all known inorganic compounds, many of which he was the first to prepare or characterize.

Berzelius's experiments led to a more complete depiction of the principles of chemical combining proportions, an area of investigation that the German chemist Jeremias Benjamin Richter named "stoichiometry" in 1792. Richter, the French chemist Joseph-Louis Proust, and the English chemist John Dalton, despite their theoretical insights, had contributed little empirical evidence toward elucidating the principles of chemical combination. By showing how compounds conformed to the laws of constant, multiple, and equivalent proportions as well as to a series of semiempirical rules devised to cover specific classes of compounds, Berzelius established the quantitative specificity by which substances combined. These results, when viewed alongside his qualitative identification of electrically opposing constituents, allowed Berzelius to specify more completely the combining properties of all known chemicals. He reported his analytical results in a series of famous publications, most prominently his *Essai sur la théorie des proportions chimiques et sur l'influence chimique de l'électricité* (1819; "Essay on the Theory of Chemical Proportions and on the Chemical Influence of Electricity"), and the atomic weight tables that appeared in the 1826 German translation of his *Lärbok i kemien* (*Textbook of Chemistry*). He continued his analytical work until 1844, reporting in specialized articles and new editions of his textbook both new results, such as his extensive analysis of the compounds of the platinum metals in 1827–28, together with refinements of his earlier experimental findings.

Atomism and Nomenclature

The project of specifying substances had several important consequences. In order to establish and display the laws of stoichiometry, Berzelius invented and perfected more exacting standards and techniques of analysis. His generalization of the older acid/base chemistry led him to extend chemical nomenclature that Lavoisier had introduced to cover the bases (mostly metallic oxides), a change that allowed Berzelius to name any compound consistently with Lavoisier's chemistry. For this purpose, he bypassed the French names that Lavoisier and his colleagues had devised as well as their translations into Swedish introduced by Berzelius's colleagues at Uppsala, Pehr Afzelius and Anders Gustav Ekeberg. Instead, Berzelius created a Latin template for translation into diverse vernacular languages.

The project of specifying substances also led Berzelius to develop a new system of notation that could portray the composition of any compound both qualitatively (by showing its electrochemically opposing ingredients) and quantitatively (by showing the proportions in which the ingredients were united). His system abbreviated the Latin names of the elements with one or two letters and applied superscripts to designate the number of atoms of each element present in both the acidic and basic ingredient. In his own work, however, Berzelius preferred to indicate the proportions of oxygen with dots placed over the letters of the oxidized elements, but most chemists rejected that practice. Instead, they followed Berzelius's younger German colleagues, who replaced his superscripts with subscripts and thus created the system still used today. Berzelius's new nomenclature and notation were prominently displayed in his 1819 *Essai*, which presented a coherent, compelling system of chemical theory backed by a vast body of analytical results that rested on improved, highly precise laboratory methods.

MINERALOGY

Berzelius applied his analytical method to two primary areas, mineralogy and organic chemistry. Both of these areas needed better ways to specify and discriminate between substances. Cultivated in Sweden for its industrial utility, mineralogy had long stimulated Berzelius's analytical interest. Berzelius himself discovered several new elements, including cerium (1803) and thorium (1828), in samples of naturally occurring minerals, and his students discovered lithium, vanadium, lanthanum, didymium (later resolved into praseodymium and neodymium), erbium (later resolved into erbium, ytterbium, scandium, holmium, and thulium), and terbium. Berzelius also discovered selenium (1818), though this element was isolated in the mud resulting from the manufacture of sulfuric acid rather than from a mineral sample. Berzelius's interest in mineralogy also fostered his analysis and preparation of new compounds of these and other elements.

Native minerals, however, were more complex in their makeup than laboratory chemicals, and therefore they were more difficult to characterize. Previous Swedish mineralogists had considered mineral species to be chemical compounds, but they had become frustrated in their attempts to discriminate one compound from another and from other mixtures. In 1813 Berzelius received a mineral collection from a visiting British physician, William MacMichael, that prompted him to take up the analysis and classification of minerals. His major contribution, reported in 1814, was recognizing that silica, formerly seen as a base, frequently served as the electronegative or acidic constituent of minerals and that the traditional mineralogical class of "earths" could be reduced primarily to silicate salts. Distinguishing mineral species therefore demanded a knowledge of the stoichiometry of complex silicates, a conviction that led Berzelius in 1815 to develop his dualistic doctrine, which now anticipated a dualistic structure for substances formerly seen as "triple salts" and for other complex minerals.

Many remaining problems in the specification of minerals were resolved by the law of isomorphism, the recognition that chemically similar substances possess similar crystal forms, discovered in 1818 by the German chemist Eilhardt Mitscherlich. Berzelius had provided both the patronage and the foundational concepts for Mitscherlich's own career. In contemporary mineralogy disputes, Berzelius frequently sided with René-Just Haüy, who based his crystallography on the existence of distinct compounds as interpreted through Lavoisier's chemistry, and against the school of Abraham Gottlob Werner, who relied on external characters such as colour, texture, and hardness to discriminate between species of minerals. Without completely subordinating mineralogy to chemistry, Berzelius transformed the field and established a flourishing tradition of chemical mineralogy.

ORGANIC CHEMISTRY

Organic chemistry also posed problems in the discrimination between substances. Berzelius originally devoted his career to physiological chemistry, a field based upon the application of chemistry and physiology to substances derived from animals and plants. To that end, he mastered traditional extractive analysis and published papers on these analyses between 1806 and 1808 that became highly regarded by his peers. However, he found that extractive analysis provided no fundamental insight into organic matter, since its products were not distinct substances but rather mixtures of broadly similar compounds. Meanwhile, his interest in organic composition was overshadowed by his forays into mineral chemistry. Only around 1814, after considerable investigation into inorganic chemistry, did he again turn his attention to organic analysis. At this point, he isolated stoichiometric compounds and worked to determine their elemental constituents. Berzelius argued that, despite differences between organic and inorganic matter, organic compounds could be assigned a dualistic composition and therefore could be specified in the same manner as inorganic ones. He improved analytical methods and, together with younger colleagues from France and Germany, fostered the advance of organic chemistry by interpreting compounds and their reactions dualistically. The application of his precept that organic chemistry could be understood in terms of the principles that govern inorganic chemistry reached its zenith in the 1830s, especially as it was embodied in the older theory of radicals. However, it was also at this time that younger chemists, including Jean-Baptiste-André Dumas and Auguste Laurent, discovered phenomena such as chlorine substitution and began to recast inorganic chemistry in the light of organic substances. Berzelius's strong resistance to this move tarnished his reputation at the close of his career and fostered pejorative assessments of his work that historians have only recently shown to be exaggerated and misleading.

A MAN OF INFLUENCE

Berzelius had a profound influence on chemistry, stemming in part from his substantial achievements and in part from his ability to enhance and project his authority. Throughout his life he cultivated professional relationships in diverse ways. He trained both Swedish students, including Nils Gabriel Sefström and Carl Gustaf Mosander, and foreign students including Heinrich Rose, Gustav Rose, and Friedrich Wöhler. He also aided the careers of protégés such as Mitscherlich. Berzelius visited foreign colleagues, meeting Davy and William Hyde Wollaston in London in 1812 and Claude-Louis Berthollet, Joseph-Louis Gay-Lussac, and Pierre-Louis Dulong in Paris in 1818 and 1819. He also maintained a vast correspondence with professional colleagues. Berzelius was equally industrious in disseminating information about his ideas, methods, and results. To this end, he published his scientific articles in French, German, and English and frequently revised his *Textbook of Chemistry* in French and German editions that were often prepared with the help of current or former students. Finally, as perpetual secretary of the Royal Swedish Academy of Sciences, he issued annual reports from 1821 to 1848 (in Swedish, German, and French) on the progress of science. These reports not only announced his major findings but also offered Olympian pronouncements that were eagerly anticipated, sometimes feared, but long highly respected.

Among Berzelius's other accomplishments were his improvements of laboratory apparatuses and techniques used for chemical and mineral analysis, especially solvent extraction, elemental analysis, quantitative wet chemistry, and qualitative mineral analysis. His mastery of technique in mineral chemistry derived from his close working relationship with the Swedish mining technologist Johan

Gottlieb Gahn, who had served as assistant to Berzelius's predecessor, Torbern Bergman. Berzelius used his textbooks and his classic, widely translated monograph *On the Use of the Blowpipe* (1820) to standardize and disseminate Gahn's methods. Berzelius also characterized and named two new concepts: "isomerism," in which chemically diverse substances possess the same composition; and "catalysis," in which certain chemical reactions are facilitated by the presence of substances that are themselves unaffected. He also coined the term *protein* while attempting to apply a dualistic organic chemistry to the constituents of living things.

NORMAN L. BOWEN

(b. June 21, 1887, Kingston, Ont., Can.—d. Sept. 11, 1956, Washington, D.C.)

Canadian geologist Norman Levi Bowen was one of the most important pioneers in the field of experimental petrology (i.e., the experimental study of the origin and chemical composition of rocks). He was widely recognized for his phase-equilibrium studies of silicate systems as they relate to the origin of igneous rocks.

Bowen studied chemistry, mineralogy, and geology at Queen's University, Kingston, Ont., earning two degrees there by 1909. He obtained his Ph.D. at the Massachusetts Institute of Technology in 1912. That year he joined the Geophysical Laboratory of the Carnegie Institution of Washington, D.C., as an assistant petrologist. He was to spend much of his career there. By 1915 Bowen had executed a group of experimental studies that proved to be critically important to petrology and formed the basis of his critical review *The Later Stages of the Evolution of the Igneous Rocks* (1915), a paper of such outstanding merit that it established Bowen's position at the age of 28 as an international figure in petrology.

Bowen resigned from the Geophysical Laboratory to return briefly to Queen's University as professor of mineralogy (1919), but after two years he returned again to the laboratory in Washington. There he remained for 16 years, broadening his attack on silicate systems. His researches carried great weight when he applied his experimental physicochemical data to field petrological problems. To this end he diligently visited classical localities relating to problems of igneous rocks: the Bushveld of South Africa, the alkalic lavas of East Africa, and the peridotites of Skye and the Fen area of Norway.

In the spring of 1927, Bowen delivered a course of lectures to advanced students in geology at Princeton University, the substance of which was published in 1928 as *The Evolution of the Igneous Rocks*. In this vigorous presentation, Bowen provided a survey and a synthesis that have exerted a profound influence on petrologic thought. Later Bowen collaborated extensively with J.F. Schairer, a young and able experimenter who had joined the laboratory from Yale University. Together they worked on silicate systems containing iron oxide, beginning with ferric oxide and later ferrous oxide.

Bowen made a second and more extended break from the Geophysical Laboratory when he taught at the University of Chicago from 1937 to 1947. He rapidly developed a school of experimental petrology there and produced a succession of papers by his pupils that dealt with equilibrium studies of alkali systems. Bowen himself presented a synthesis of these results in their bearing on the origin and differentiation of alkaline rocks (1945).

After World War II, Bowen was induced to return once more to the Geophysical Laboratory in 1947 to cooperate in research on mineral systems embracing volatiles, particularly water. This work culminated in studies (published in 1958), with O.F. Tuttle as a collaborator, on the granite system.

Bowen's association with the Geophysical Laboratory extended, in all, more than 35 years, and his long and splendid record was recognized by the award of honours from learned societies in the United States and Europe. He retired in 1952 but was still active and had an office in the Geophysical Laboratory as research associate until his death.

JAMES DWIGHT DANA

(b. Feb. 12, 1813, Utica, N.Y., U.S. — d. April 14, 1895, New Haven, Conn.)

James Dwight Dana was an American geologist, mineralogist, and naturalist who, in explorations of the South Pacific, the U.S. Northwest, Europe, and elsewhere, made important studies of mountain building, volcanic activity, sea life, and the origin and structure of continents and ocean basins.

Dana attended Charles Bartlett's Academy, then entered Yale College as a sophomore in 1830. On graduation from Yale in 1833 he instructed midshipmen in mathematics on a U.S. Navy cruise to the Mediterranean; he returned to New Haven in 1836 as an assistant to his former teacher, Benjamin Silliman, professor of chemistry and mineralogy at Yale. Evidence of Dana's great productive energy came at age 24 with the publication in 1837 of *A System of Mineralogy,* a work of 580 pages that has persisted through numerous editions.

In 1838 Dana joined a United States exploring expedition to the South Seas with Charles Wilkes; he served four years as a geologist and also was responsible for much of the zoological work. In 1844, two years after his return from that expedition, Dana married Henrietta Silliman, the daughter of his mentor at Yale, and settled in New Haven. Dana spent his intense energy largely on science. From 1844 to 1854, his most productive years, he published about 7,000 printed pages in addition to hundreds of plates, most of which he drew. His writings on the Wilkes expedition include four illustrated quarto volumes and numerous short papers.

The main thrust of Dana's effort was geological. Among his many publications were the text *Manual of Mineralogy* (1848) and three editions of *A System of Mineralogy* (1st ed., 1837), including a complete revision in which he founded a classification of minerals based on mathematics, physics, and chemistry. More significant to Dana's impact on American geology during this decade was the start of his long association with the *American Journal of Science,* a leading organ of scientific inquiry founded by Benjamin Silliman. As an editor and contributor of critical reviews, original papers, and perceptive syntheses, Dana exerted a vitalizing influence on American geology. One of the best-informed men of science in his day, his concern with the physical processes that produced geologic phenomena led to brilliant generalizations on such fundamental questions as the formation of the physical features of Earth, the origin and structure of continents and ocean basins, the nature of mountain building, and volcanic activity. From his own studies and his mastery of the works of other American and foreign geologists, Dana constructed a view of Earth as a geologic unity developing through time. Adopting the theory of a contracting Earth cooling from a molten condition, he argued that the present continents mark areas that cooled first; subsequent contractions caused the intervening oceanic areas to subside. As settling oceanic crusts adapted periodically to a shrinking interior, pressure was exerted against continental margins causing upheaval of great mountain chains such as the Appalachians, Rockies, and Andes. Dana stressed the progressive change of Earth's physical features but at first was reluctant to accept the idea of the evolution of living things.

By the early 1850s Dana had attained international recognition and was corresponding with other outstanding scientists of his day, among them Asa Gray, noted American botanist; Louis Agassiz, Swiss-born naturalist and teacher at Harvard; and Charles Darwin. All had measurable influence on his thinking. Spurred by tentative proposals from Harvard for Dana's services, friends at Yale established the Silliman Professorship of Natural History, which Dana accepted in 1856. But in 1859, the strain of his self-imposed overwork resulted in a physical breakdown from which he never fully recovered. During his remaining 35 years he was forced to live a secluded existence, largely withdrawn from the public. For a less modest man this would have been difficult, for many academic honours came to him during this period. Recognition included the presidencies of the American Association for the Advancement

James D. Dana. Library of Congress, Washington, D.C. (Digital File Number: cph 3a28456)

of Science and the Geological Society of America; he was also a founding member of the National Academy of Sciences.

Despite ill health Dana continued to publish: in 1862 his influential textbook, *Manual of Geology* (4 eds.); in 1864 *A Text-book of Geology,* a more elementary work; and in 1872 *Corals and Coral Islands,* which was the climax to his notable studies of coral reefs, begun on the Wilkes expedition. Dana investigated coral islands in greater detail than anyone before him, substantiating Darwin's observation that atolls were evidence of subsidence of the ocean bottom. Reef-building corals, Dana independently concluded, lived only in shallow, tropical waters on hard substrates, commonly forming fringing reefs about volcanic islands. Coral rock found at some depth on island flanks and atolls made only of reef rock indicated that extensive volcanic lands had disappeared beneath the Pacific leaving clusters of atolls to mark their former existence.

During his later years he wrestled with the challenge of organic evolution proposed by Darwin. Always a deeply religious man, Dana believed in the special creation of species, yet he was keenly aware of the intricate relationships between species and their environment. Darwin's impressive argument, coupled with Dana's own zoological knowledge, was persuasive in the end, however, and he adopted evolution theory in the last edition of his *Manual.* For Dana the natural and the divine had to be inseparable—all nature and the design of continual improvement of life that he read into it were a manifestation of the divine.

During Dana's lifetime, and largely under his leadership, American geology grew from a collection and classification of unrelated facts into a mature science.

CLARENCE EDWARD DUTTON

(b. May 15, 1841, Wallingford, Conn., U.S.—d. Jan. 4, 1912, Englewood, N.J.)

American geologist and pioneer seismologist Clarence Edward Dutton developed and named the principle of isostasy. According to this principle, the level of Earth's crust is determined by its density; lighter material rises, forming continents, mountains, and plateaus, and heavier material sinks, forming basins and ocean floors.

Clarence Edward Dutton. National Oceanic and Atmospheric Administration (Image ID: pers00069)

Dutton joined the U.S. Army as a second lieutenant in 1862. After the Civil War, he developed an interest in geology. In 1875 he joined the naturalist John Wesley Powell in the U.S. Geographical and Geological Survey of the Rocky Mountain region and spent 10 years exploring the plateaus of Utah, Arizona, and New Mexico. There he investigated volcanic action and the uplifting, sinking, twisting, and folding of Earth's crust.

Dutton's study of the earthquake that affected Charleston, S.C., in 1886 led him to publish a report (1889) in which he advanced a method for determining the depth of the focal point of an earthquake and for measuring with unprecedented accuracy the velocity of waves. He proposed his principle of isostasy in the paper "On Some of the Greater Problems of Physical Geology" (1892). In 1904 he published the semipopular treatise *Earthquakes in the Light of the New Seismology*. Late in his career Dutton concluded that lava is liquefied by the heat released during decay of radioactive elements and that it is forced to the surface by the weight of overlying rocks.

JAMES HALL

(b. Sept. 12, 1811, Hingham, Mass., U.S.—d. Aug. 7, 1898, Bethlehem, N.H.)

James Hall was an American geologist and paleontologist who was a major contributor to the geosynclinal theory of mountain building. According to this theory, sediment buildup in a shallow basin causes the basin to sink, thus forcing the neighbouring area to rise. His detailed studies established the stratigraphy of eastern North America.

Even as a student, Hall spent his summers and limited finances doing fieldwork, including the collection and identification of more than 900 species of plants. He became an assistant professor at Rensselaer Polytechnic Institute, Rensselaer, N.Y., in 1832 and later professor of chemistry, natural science, and geology.

In 1836 he was appointed state geologist for the Geological Survey of New York. Assigned to the western district, he conducted studies that culminated in his massive report *Geology of New York* (part 4, 1843), a classic in American geology. Although he could not explain the uplift of the sedimentary beds that formed the Appalachians, his observations were instrumental in forming the geosynclinal theory.

Hall became director of the Museum of Natural History, Albany, N.Y., in 1871. His 13-volume *The Palaeontology of New York* (1847–94) contained the results of his exhaustive studies of the Silurian and Devonian (approximately 360 million to 415 million years old) fossils found in New York.

He was state geologist of Iowa from 1855 to 1858 and of Wisconsin from 1857 to 1860. His publications included more than 260 scientific papers and 35 books dealing with numerous phases of the geology and paleontology of the United States and Canada. He was a charter member of the National Academy of Sciences.

RENÉ-JUST HAÜY

(b. Feb. 28, 1743, Saint-Just-en-Chaussée, France — d. June 1, 1822, Paris)

René-Just-Haüy was a French mineralogist and one of the founders of the science of crystallography.

After studying theology, Haüy became an abbé and for 21 years served as professor at the Collège de Navarre. In 1802 he became professor of mineralogy at the Museum of Natural History in Paris, and in 1809 he was appointed to a similar post at the Sorbonne.

His interest in crystallography resulted, he later reported, from the accidental breaking of a piece of calcite. In examining the fragments he discovered that they cleaved along straight planes that met at constant angles. He broke more pieces of calcite and found that, regardless of the original shape, the broken fragments were consistently rhombohedral. From subsequent experiments he derived a thoroughgoing theory of crystal structure. Fundamental to his theory were the laws of decrement and of constancy of angles, whereby the cleavage forms of crystals were related geometrically to their primary forms or nuclei. Haüy subsequently applied his theory to the classification of minerals. He was also known for his studies of pyroelectricity and piezoelectricity in crystals. His publications include *Traité de miné ra logie* (1801;

"Treatise on Mineralogy"), *Traité de physique* ("Treatise on Physics"), written at Napoleon's request (1803), and *Tableau comparatif* ("Comparative Table"), his mineralogical classification (1809).

ROBERT HOOKE

(b. July 18, 1635, Freshwater, Isle of Wight, Eng.—d. March 3, 1703, London)

Robert Hooke was an English physicist who discovered the law of elasticity, known as Hooke's law. He was also known for his research in a remarkable variety of fields.

In 1655 Hooke was employed by Robert Boyle to construct the Boylean air pump. Five years later, Hooke discovered his law of elasticity, which states that the stretching of a solid body (e.g., metal, wood) is proportional to the force applied to it. The law laid the basis for studies of stress and strain and for understanding of elastic materials. He applied these studies in his designs for the balance springs of watches. In 1662 he was appointed curator of experiments to the Royal Society of London and was elected a fellow the following year.

One of the first men to build a Gregorian reflecting telescope, Hooke discovered the fifth star in the Trapezium, an asterism in the constellation Orion, in 1664 and first suggested that Jupiter rotates on its axis. His detailed sketches of Mars were used in the 19th century to determine that planet's rate of rotation. In 1665 he was appointed professor of geometry in Gresham College. In *Micrographia* (1665; "Small Drawings") he included his studies and illustrations of the crystal structure of snowflakes, discussed the possibility of manufacturing artificial fibres by a process similar to the spinning of the silkworm, and first used the word *cell* to name the microscopic honeycomb cavities in cork. His studies of microscopic fossils led him to become one of the first proponents of a theory of evolution.

He suggested that the force of gravity could be measured by utilizing the motion of a pendulum (1666) and attempted to show that Earth and the Moon follow an elliptical path around the Sun. In 1672 he discovered the phenomenon of diffraction (the bending of light rays around corners); to explain it, he offered the wave theory of light. He stated the inverse square law to describe planetary motions in 1678, a law that Newton later used in modified form. Hooke complained that he was not given sufficient credit for the law and became involved in bitter controversy with Newton. Hooke was the first man to state in general that all matter expands when heated and that air is made up of particles separated from each other by relatively large distances.

JAMES HUTTON

(b. June 3, 1726, Edinburgh, Scot.—d. March 26, 1797, Edinburgh)

James Hutton was a Scottish geologist, chemist, naturalist, and originator of one of the fundamental principles of geology—uniformitarianism, which explains the features of Earth's crust by means of natural processes over geologic time.

Hutton was the son of a merchant and city officeholder. Though Hutton's father died when his son was quite young, Hutton managed an education in the local grammar school and at the University of Edinburgh. Although already interested in chemistry, he entered the legal profession. But as a lawyer's apprentice, he is said to have devoted more time to amusing his fellow clerks with chemical experiments than to copying legal documents. He, along with his friend James Davie, was also deeply interested in investigating the manufacture of sal ammoniac from coal soot. As a result, he was released from law apprenticeship before his first year was out, and he turned to the study of medicine, as it was most closely related to chemistry. He spent three years at the University of Edinburgh, then two in Paris, and finally was granted an M.D. degree in Holland in September 1749.

But medicine held small appeal for Hutton. His association with Davie in developing an inexpensive method for the manufacture of sal ammoniac proved financially rewarding, and so Hutton decided to take up farming in Berwickshire, Scot. By 1765 both the farm and the company producing sal ammoniac were prospering, and with a good income available, he gave up farming in 1768 to establish himself in Edinburgh, where he could pursue his scientific interests.

Hutton devoted his time to extensive scientific reading and traveled widely to inspect rocks and observe the actions of natural processes. His chief contribution to scientific knowledge, the uniformitarian principle, was put forward in his papers presented to the Royal Society of Edinburgh in 1785. Two of these papers were published in 1788 in the *Transactions of the Royal Society of Edinburgh* under the title "Theory of the Earth; or an Investigation of the Laws Observable in the Composition, Dissolution, and Restoration of Land Upon the Globe."

Hutton's view as stated in these papers was that the world's geologic phenomena can be explained in terms of observable processes, and that those processes now at work on and within Earth have operated with general uniformity over immensely long periods of time. These two papers marked a turning point for geology; from that time on, geology became a science founded upon the principle of uniformitarianism.

Hutton's ideas were astonishing when viewed in the context of the opinion of his day. By the late 18th century, much knowledge had been gained about rocks, strata, and fossils, but none of this wealth of data had been synthesized into a workable general theory of geology. Such a task was seriously impeded by the still-accepted belief that Earth had been created only about 6,000 years ago, according to the narrative in the biblical book of Genesis. The world's sedimentary rocks were believed by some geologists to have been formed when immense quantities of minerals precipitated out of the waters of the biblical flood. Erosional processes had long been recognized, but there was no equivalent explanation for the creation of land surfaces, as opposed to their destruction by erosion. The significance of rock formation by means of volcanism and other heat-generated processes in Earth's crust was almost completely unrecognized, as was the existence of igneous rocks in general.

Hutton's ideas were diametrically opposed to much of this contemporary theory. He asserted that many rocks had indeed been formed by sedimentary processes—i.e., that rock particles had been washed off the land into the oceans, had accumulated in beds there, and had solidified into rocks. But he posited that the solidification into rocks was due not to the particles' simple precipitation out of a watery solution but rather was due to the effects of pressure and heat, an explanation which stands to the present day. Hutton asserted that the wearing down of land surfaces by erosion was countered by the formation of new land surfaces due to volcanism and other processes in which the internal heat of Earth brought new rock constitutents up to Earth's surface. These new mountains and other landforms were then in turn eroded and were deposited as sediments in the sea, from which they could be upthrust into new land surfaces by subterranean heat-generated processes.

Hutton claimed that the totality of these geologic processes could fully explain the current landforms all over the world, and no biblical explanations were necessary in this regard. Finally, he stated that the processes of erosion, deposition, sedimentation, and upthrusting were cyclical and must have been repeated many times in Earth's history. Given the enormous spans of time taken by such cycles, Hutton asserted that the age of Earth must be inconceivably great.

Hutton summarized his views and provided ample observational evidence for his conclusions in a work published in two volumes, *Theory of the Earth*, in 1795. A third volume was partly finished at the time of Hutton's death.

Although Hutton's ideas received a fairly wide circulation among European scientists, their immediate impact was blunted by the fact that Hutton's writing style was difficult to understand. Fortunately, his close friend John Playfair wrote a clear and precise condensation of Hutton's work, embellished with additional observations of his own, and published it in 1802 under the title *Illustrations of the Huttonian Theory of the Earth*. It went far toward establishing the correctness of uniformitarianism, the cornerstone on which the science of geology is erected.

SIR CHARLES LYELL

(b. Nov. 14, 1797, Kinnordy, Forfarshire, Scot. — d. Feb. 22, 1875, London, Eng.)

Scottish geologist Charles Lyell was largely responsible for the general acceptance of the view that all features of Earth's surface are produced by physical, chemical, and biological processes through long periods of geological time. The concept was called uniformitarianism (initially set forth by James Hutton). Lyell's achievements laid the foundations for evolutionary biology as well as for an understanding of Earth's development. He was knighted in 1848 and made a baronet in 1864.

LIFE

Lyell was born at Kinnordy, the stately family home at the foot of the Grampian Mountains in eastern Scotland. His principal childhood associations, however, were with the New Forest near Southampton, Eng., where his parents moved before he was two years old. His father, a naturalist who later turned to more literary pursuits, kept the study well stocked with books on every subject, including geology. The eldest of 10 children, Charles attended a series of private schools, where he was not a particularly diligent student; he much preferred rambles in the New Forest and his father's instruction at home to those places, with their schoolboy pranks and pecking orders whose spirit he never really shared. His first scientific hobby was collecting butterflies and aquatic insects, an activity pursued intensively for some years, even though labelled unmanly by local residents. His observations went far beyond those of any ordinary boy, and later this instinct for collecting and comparing led to important discoveries.

At 19 Lyell entered Oxford University, where his interest in classics, mathematics, and geology was stimulated, the latter by the enthusiastic lectures of William Buckland, later widely known for his attempt to prove Noah's Flood by studies of fossils from cave deposits. Lyell spent the long vacations between terms travelling and conducting geological studies. Notes made in 1817 on the origin of the Yarmouth lowlands clearly foreshadow his later work.

The penetrating geological and cultural observations Lyell made while on a continental tour with his family in 1818 were as remarkable as the number of miles he walked in a day. In December 1819 he earned a B.A. with honours and moved to London to study law.

CAREER

Lyell's eyes were weakened by hard law study, and he sought and found relief by spending much time on geological work outdoors. Among these holidays was a visit to Sussex in 1822 to see evidence of vertical movements of Earth's crust. In 1823, on a visit to Paris, he met the renowned naturalists Alexander von Humboldt and Georges Cuvier and examined the Paris Basin with the French geologist Louis-Constant Prévost. In 1824 Lyell studied sediments forming in freshwater lakes near Kinnordy. When in London, Lyell participated in its vigorous intellectual life, meeting such literati as Sir Walter Scott and taking active part in several scientific societies.

NEW APPROACH TO GEOLOGY

Prodded to finish his law studies, Lyell was admitted to the bar in 1825, but with his father's financial support he practiced geology more than law, publishing his first scientific papers that year. Lyell was rapidly developing new principles of reasoning in geology and began to plan a book which would stress that there are natural (as opposed to supernatural) explanations for all geologic phenomena, that the ordinary natural processes of today and their products do not differ in kind or magnitude from those of the past, and that Earth must therefore be very ancient because these everyday processes work so slowly. With the ambitious young geologist Roderick Murchison, he explored districts in France and Italy where proof of his principles could be sought. From northern Italy Lyell went south alone to Sicily. Poor roads and accommodations made travel difficult, but in the region around Mt. Etna he found striking confirmation of his belief in the adequacy of natural causes to explain the features of Earth and in the great antiquity even of such a recent feature as Etna itself.

The results of this trip, which lasted from May 1828 until February 1829, far exceeded Lyell's expectations. Returning to London, he set to work immediately on his book, *Principles of Geology,* the first volume of which was published in July 1830. A reader today may wonder why this book filled with facts purports to deal with principles. Lyell had to teach his principles through masses of facts and examples because in 1830 his method of scientific inquiry was novel and even mildly heretical. A remark of Charles Darwin shows how brilliantly Lyell succeeded: "The very first place which I examined...showed me clearly the wonderful superiority of Lyell's manner of treating geology, compared with that of any other author, whose work I had with me or ever afterwards read."

During the summer of 1830 Lyell travelled through the geologically complex Pyrenees to Spain, where the closed, repressed society both fascinated and repelled him. Returning to France, he was astonished to find King Charles X dethroned, the tricolour everywhere, and geologists able to talk only of politics. Back in London he set to work again on the *Principles of Geology,* finishing Volume II in December 1831 and the third and final volume in April 1833. His steady work was relieved by occasional social or scientific gatherings and a trip to a volcanic district in Germany close to the home of his sweetheart, Mary Horner, in Bonn, whom he married in July 1832, taking a long honeymoon and geological excursion in Switzerland

and Italy. Mary, whose father had geological leanings, shared Charles's interests. For 40 years she was his closest companion; the happiness of their marriage increased because of her ability to participate in his work.

During the next eight years the Lyells led a quiet life. Winters were devoted to study, scientific and social activities, and revision of *Principles of Geology,* which sold so well that new editions were frequently required. Data for the new editions were gathered during summer travels, including two visits to Scandinavia in 1834 and 1837. In 1832 and 1833 Lyell delivered well-received lectures at King's College, London, afterward resigning the professorship as too time-consuming.

SCIENTIFIC EMINENCE

Publication of the *Principles of Geology* placed him among the recognized leaders of his field, compelling him to devote more time to scientific affairs. During these years he gained the friendship of men like Darwin and the astronomer Sir John Herschel. In 1838 Lyell's *Elements of Geology* was published; it described European rocks and fossils from the most recent, Lyell's specialty, to the oldest then known. Like the *Principles of Geology,* this well-illustrated work was periodically enlarged and updated.

In 1841 Lyell accepted an invitation to lecture and travel for a year in North America, returning again for nine months in 1845–46 and for two short visits in the 1850s. During their travels, the Lyells visited nearly every part of the United States east of the Mississippi River and much of eastern Canada, seeing almost all of the important geological "monuments" along the way, including Niagara Falls. Lyell was amazed at the comparative ease of travel, although they saw many places newly claimed from the wilderness. A veteran of coach and sail days, Lyell often praised the speed and comfort of the new railroads and steamships. Lyell's lectures at the Lowell Institute in Boston attracted thousands of people of both sexes and every social station. Lyell wrote enthusiastic and informative books, in 1845 and 1849, about each of his two long visits to the New World. Unlike the majority of well-off Victorians, Lyell was a vocal supporter of the Union cause in the American Civil War. Familiar with both North and South, he admired the bravery and military skill of the South but believed in the necessity and inevitability of a Northern victory.

In the 1840s Lyell became more widely known outside the scientific community, socializing with Lord John Russell, a leading Whig; Sir Robert Peel, founder of Scotland Yard; and Thomas Macaulay, the historian of England. In 1848 Lyell was knighted for his scientific achievements, beginning a long and friendly acquaintance with the royal family. He studied the prevention of mine disasters with the English physicist Michael Faraday in 1844, served as a commissioner for the Great Exhibition in 1851–52, and in the same year helped to begin educational reform at Oxford University—he had long objected to church domination of British colleges. Lyell's professional reputation continued to grow; during his lifetime he received many awards and honorary degrees, including, in 1858, the Copley Medal, the highest award of the Royal Society of London; and he was many times president of various scientific societies or functions. Expanding reputation and responsibilities brought no letup in his geological explorations. With Mary, he travelled in Europe or Britain practically every summer, visiting Madeira in the winter of 1854 to study the origin of the island itself and of its curious fauna and flora. Lyell especially liked to visit young geologists, from whom he felt "old stagers" had much to learn. After exhaustive restudy carried out on muleback in

1858, he proved conclusively that Mt. Etna had been built up by repeated small eruptions rather than by a cataclysmic upheaval as some geologists still insisted. He wrote Mary that "a good mule is like presenting an old geologist with a young pair of legs."

In 1859 publication of Darwin's *Origin of Species* gave new impetus to Lyell's work. Although Darwin drew heavily on Lyell's *Principles of Geology* both for style and content, Lyell had never shared his protégé's belief in evolution. But reading the *Origin of Species* triggered studies that culminated in publication of *The Geological Evidence of the Antiquity of Man* in 1863, in which Lyell tentatively accepted evolution by natural selection. Only during completion of a major revision of the *Principles of Geology* in 1865 did he fully adopt Darwin's conclusions, however, adding powerful arguments of his own that won new adherents to Darwin's theory. Why Lyell was hesitant in accepting Darwinism is best explained by Darwin himself: "Considering his age, his former views, and position in society, I think his action has been heroic."

After 1865 Lyell's activities became more restricted as his strength waned, although he never entirely gave up outdoor geology. His wife, 12 years his junior, died unexpectedly in 1873 after a short illness, leaving Lyell to write, "I endeavour by daily work at my favourite science, to forget as far as possible the dreadful change which this has made in my existence." He died in 1875, while revising his *Principles of Geology* for its 12th edition, and was buried in Westminster Abbey.

ASSESSMENT

Lyell typified his times in beginning as an amateur geologist and becoming a professional by study and experience. Unlike most geologists then and now, however, he never considered observations and collections as ends in themselves but used them to build and test theories. The *Principles of Geology* opened up new vistas of time and change for the younger group of scientists around Darwin. Only after they were gone did Lyell's reputation begin to diminish, largely at the hands of critics who had not read the *Principles of Geology* as carefully as had Darwin and attributed to Darwin things he had learned from Lyell. Lyell is still underestimated by some geologists who fail to see that the methods and principles they use every day actually originated with Lyell and were revolutionary in his era. The lasting value of Lyell's work and its importance for the modern reader are clear in Darwin's assessment:

> *The great merit of the Principles was that it altered the whole tone of one's mind, and therefore that, when seeing a thing never seen by Lyell, one yet saw it partially through his eyes.*

JOHN MILNE

(b. Dec. 30, 1850, Liverpool, Eng.—d. July 30, 1913, Shide, Isle of Wight)

An English geologist and influential seismologist, John Milne developed the modern seismograph and promoted the establishment of seismological stations worldwide.

Milne worked as a mining engineer in Labrador and Newfoundland, Can., and in 1874 served as geologist on the expedition led by Charles T. Beke, the noted British explorer and biblical scholar, to Egypt and northwestern Arabia. In 1875 Milne accepted the position of professor of geology and mining at the Imperial College of Engineering, Tokyo. He designed one of the first reliable seismographs in 1880 and traveled widely in Japan to set up 968 seismological stations for a survey of Japan's widespread earthquakes. After many seminal earthquake studies, Milne returned to England in 1894 and established a private seismological station near Newport, Isle of Wight. His attempt in 1906 to determine the velocity of seismic waves through Earth was largely unsuccessful. He served as secretary of the Seismological Committee of the British Association and organized a worldwide network of observation stations. Many of his findings were published in his books *Earthquakes* (1883) and *Seismology* (1898).

JOHN PLAYFAIR

(b. March 10, 1748, Benvie, Forfarshire, Scot.—d. July 20, 1819, Burntisland, Fife)

John Playfair, engraving, 1875. Photos .com/Jupiter Images

John Playfair was a Scottish geologist and mathematician known for his explanation and expansion of ideas on uniformitarianism—the theory that Earth's features generally represent a response to former processes similar in kind to processes that are operative today.

A professor of natural philosophy at the University of Edinburgh, Playfair was the first to propose that a river cuts its own valley and was also the first to recognize the transport role of glaciers. He wrote *Elements of Geometry* (1795),

Illustrations of the Huttonian Theory of the Earth (1802), and *Outlines of Natural Philosophy* (1812–16).

JOHN WESLEY POWELL

(b. March 24, 1834, Mount Morris, N.Y., U.S.—d. Sept. 23, 1902, Haven, Maine)

John Wesley Powell was an American geologist and ethnologist who published the first classification of American Indian languages and was the first director of the U.S. Bureau of Ethnology.

After fighting in the American Civil War, Powell joined Illinois Wesleyan University as professor of geology. In 1867 he became a lecturer at Illinois Normal College (now Illinois State University at Normal) and began a series of expeditions to the Rocky Mountains and the canyons of the Green and Colorado rivers. From 1871 to 1879 he directed a federal geologic and geographic survey of western lands in the public domain and encouraged the government to initiate land-utilization projects. During this period he published three major works. In *Exploration of the Colorado River of the West and Its Tributaries* (1875; rev. ed., *Canyons of Colorado,* 1895), he originated and formalized a number of concepts that became part of the standard working vocabulary of geology. His *Introduction to the Study of Indian Languages* (1877) firmly established him as an anthropologist. It contained a linguistic classification of Indian languages and grouped words according to use and emotion. Powell's *Report on the Lands of the Arid Region of the United States* (1878; reprinted 1962) is regarded as a landmark in conservation literature.

When the U.S. Bureau of Ethnology of the Smithsonian Institution, Washington, D.C., was established in 1879,

Powell became its first director and remained with it until his death. Continuing the study of Indian ethnology and languages, he published the first complete and still-authoritative classification and distribution map of 58 language stocks of the United States and Canada (1891). Powell also served as director of the U.S. Geological Survey (1881–92), working extensively on the mapping of water sources and advancing irrigation projects.

WILLIAM SMITH

(b. March 23, 1769, Churchill, Oxfordshire, Eng.—d. Aug. 28, 1839, Northampton, Northamptonshire)

William Smith, engraving, 1875.
Photos.com/Jupiter Images

English engineer and geologist William Smith is best known for his development of the science of stratigraphy. Smith's great geologic map of England and Wales (1815) set the style for modern geologic maps, and many of the colourful names he applied to the strata are still in use today.

Smith was the son of an Oxfordshire blacksmith of farming stock. Only seven when his father died, Smith was cared for by a farming uncle. He attended a village school, learned the basic methods of surveying from books he bought himself, and collected the abundant fossils of his native Cotswold hills. In 1787 he became an assistant to Edward Webb, a surveyor in nearby Stow-on-the-Wold, who in 1791 helped Smith become established in the Somersetshire coal district southwest of Bath. The steam locomotive had not yet been invented, and canal-building was at its height, particularly for the transportation of coal. There was also abundant work in the enclosure and drainage of fields.

During preliminary surveys for a proposed Somersetshire Coal Canal in 1793, Smith discovered that the strata outcropping in the northern part of the region dip regularly eastward, like so many "slices of bread and butter." On a long trip in 1794 to examine canals and collieries, he had an opportunity to extend his observations. His suspicion that the strata of Somerset could be traced far northward across England was brilliantly confirmed as the familiar beds were encountered again and again during this journey. Excavation of the new canal began in 1795, and Smith, studying the fresh cuts, found that each stratum contained "fossils peculiar to itself."

His work on the canal continued until 1799, when he was abruptly dismissed, probably over an engineering dispute. But Smith had a good reputation in Bath, at that time a major intellectual and social centre, and quickly built a far-flung business as a geological engineer. In 1804 he moved his business headquarters to a house in London, where his fossil collection and geologic maps were always on display.

In 1799 Smith dictated to an amateur geologist in Bath his now-famous table of strata in the vicinity of Bath, which became a principal means for circulating his revolutionary discoveries. He also exhibited his maps and stratigraphic sections at agricultural fairs, such as the Holkham "Sheepshearings," which he regularly attended.

Much of his professional work was for the gentleman farmers who supported these shows, but he also supervised major reclamation projects in Norfolk and Wales, restoration of the hot springs at Bath, and a multitude of canal and colliery projects, sometimes travelling 10,000 miles a year (an incredible total made possible by the inauguration of fast mail coaches in 1784).

Smith's intelligence and practical knowledge of geology and groundwater took him to the front rank of his profession, but he never became wealthy because of his personal objective: mapping the geology of England. He always made copious notes of what he saw on the job and spent all his extra time and money on side trips to fill in blank spaces on his map, often sleeping in the coach on the way to his next appointment. Where exposures were few, he used soil, topography, and vegetation to identify underlying rock. His epochal geologic map of England and Wales appeared in 1815 under the title *A Delineation of the Strata of England and Wales, with Part of Scotland*. This was followed by an excellent series of county maps between 1819 and 1824.

During these years, Smith was in financial straits, undoubtedly exacerbated by the agricultural depression that followed the Napoleonic Wars. Failure of a quarry in Somerset lost him the property and forced the sale of his fossil collection to the British Museum in London. When creditors seized his London property after he had spent 10 weeks in debtor's prison in 1819, he sold out and left for Yorkshire. For some years he had no permanent home but finally settled in Scarborough among a small band of geological enthusiasts, one of whom retained him as a consultant on his nearby estate. Recognition of his achievements came from other sources. In 1822 his work was praised by William D. Conybeare and William Phillips in their textbook on English stratigraphy, *Outlines of the*

Geology of England and Wales. In 1831 he received from the Geological Society of London the first Wollaston Medal and in 1832 a yearly pension from the crown. He died in 1839 on his way to a scientific meeting in Birmingham.

Smith was not only exceptionally observant but possessed the power to integrate his observations. He saw that different rock layers contained different fossils and used this fact to trace strata over hundreds of miles. So great was his ability that geologists still use all of the techniques he introduced, and current geologic maps of England differ from his primarily in detail. Between 1815 and 1817 he published a few thin volumes on his work, but in a sense they were too late. Smith had always talked freely to anyone interested, and his knowledge was already public property being applied by geologists in every part of Britain. The fame Smith achieved in his lifetime remains undimmed to this day, and he is universally admired as the "Founder of Stratigraphy."

NICOLAUS STENO

(b. Jan. 10, 1638, Copenhagen, Den.—d. Nov. 26, 1686, Schwerin [Germany])

Nicolaus Steno (Danish: Niels Steensen or Niels Stensen) was a geologist and anatomist whose early observations greatly advanced the development of geology.

In 1660 Steno went to Amsterdam to study human anatomy, and while there he discovered the parotid salivary duct, also called Stensen's duct. In 1665 he went to Florence, where he was appointed physician to the grand duke Ferdinand II.

Steno traveled extensively in Italy, and in 1669 he published his geological observations in *De solido intra solidum naturaliter contento dissertationis prodromus* (*The Prodromus of*

Nicolaus Steno's Dissertation Concerning a Solid Body Enclosed by Process of Nature Within a Solid). In this work, a milestone in the literature of geology, he laid the foundations of the science of crystallography. He reported that, although quartz crystals differ greatly in physical appearance, they all have the same angles between corresponding faces. In addition he proposed the revolutionary idea that fossils are the remains of ancient living organisms and that many rocks are the result of sedimentation.

Steno was the first to realize that Earth's crust contains a chronological history of geologic events and that the history may be deciphered by careful study of the strata and fossils. He rejected the idea that mountains grow like trees, proposing instead that they are formed by alterations of Earth's crust. Hampered by religious intolerance and dogma, Steno was constrained to place all of geologic history within a 6,000-year span.

Upon becoming a Roman Catholic in 1667, Steno abandoned science for religion. He took holy orders in 1675, was made a bishop in 1677, and was appointed apostolic vicar of northern Germany and Scandinavia.

STRABO

(b. 64/63 BCE, Amaseia, Pontus—d. 23 CE, ?)

Strabo was a Greek geographer and historian whose *Geography* is the only extant work covering the whole range of peoples and countries known to both Greeks and Romans during the reign of Augustus (27 BCE–14 CE). Its numerous quotations from technical literature, moreover, provide a remarkable account of the state of Greek geographical science, as well as of the history of the countries it surveys.

Strabo belonged on his mother's side to a famous family, whose members had held important offices under Mithradates V (around 150–120 BCE), as well as under Mithradates the Great, the opponent of Rome (132–63 BCE). His first teacher was the master of rhetoric Aristodemus, a former tutor of the sons of Pompey (106–48 BCE) in Nysa (now Sultanhisar in Turkey) on the Maeander. He moved to Rome in 44 BCE to study with Tyrannion, the former tutor of Cicero, and with Xenarchus, both of whom were members of the Aristotelian school of philosophy. Under the influence of Athenodorus, former tutor of Octavius, who probably introduced him into the future emperor's circle, he turned toward Stoical philosophy, the precepts of which included the view that one unique principle ceaselessly pervading the whole universe causes all phenomena.

It was in Rome, where he stayed at least until 31 BCE, that he wrote his first major works, his 47-book *Historical Sketches,* published around 20 BCE, of which but a few quotations survive. A vast and eclectic compilation, it was meant as a continuation of Polybius' *Histories.* The *Historical Sketches* covered the history of the known world from 145 BCE—that is, from the conquest of Greece by the Romans— to the Battle of Actium (31

Strabo, 15th-century woodcut. Photos.com/ Jupiterimages

BCE), or to the beginnings of the principate of the Roman emperor Augustus (27 BCE).

In 29 BCE, Strabo visited the island of Gyaros (today known as Yiáros, or Nisós) in the Aegean Sea, on his way to Corinth, Greece, where Augustus was staying. In 25 or 24, together with Aelius Gallus, prefect of Egypt, who had been sent on a military mission to Arabia, he sailed up the Nile as far as Philae. There are then no further references to him until 17 CE, when he attended the triumph of the Roman general Germanicus Caesar (15 BCE to 19 CE) in Rome. He died after having devoted his last years to compiling his second important work, his *Geographical Sketches*. Judging by the date when he wrote his personal notes, he must have worked on the book after his stay in Egypt and then have put it aside from 2(?) BCE to 14 CE, when he started the final edition, which he brought to an end in 23 CE.

The first two books, in effect, provide a definition of the aims and methods of geography by criticizing earlier works and authors. Strabo found fault with the map designing of the Greek scholar Eratosthenes, who lived from *c.* 276 to *c.* 194 BCE; Eratosthenes had combined astronomical data with coast and road measurements, but Strabo found his work lacking in precision. Although Strabo closely followed the treatise against Eratosthenes of the Greek astronomer Hipparchus, who had lived in the 2nd century BCE, he blamed Hipparchus for neglecting the description of Earth. On the other hand, he appreciated Polybius, who, in addition to his historical works, had written two books on European geography that Strabo admired for their descriptions of places and peoples. Although he praised Posidonius, the Greek historian and philosopher who lived from about 135 to 51 BCE, for his knowledge of physical geography and ethnography, he rejected Posidonius' theory of climatic zones and particularly his hypothesis that the equatorial zone was habitable. This critical study led him logically to decide in favour of a descriptive type of geography, based on a map with an orthogonal (perpendicular) projection. The problem of projecting the sphere on a flat surface is not dealt with at any length, for his work, as he said, was not designed for mathematicians but for statesmen who must know countries, natural resources, and customs.

In books III to VI, Strabo described successively Iberia, Gaul, and Italy, for which his main sources were Polybius and Posidonius, both of whom had visited these countries; in addition, Artemidorus, a Greek geographer born around 140 BCE and author of a book describing a voyage around the inhabited Earth, provided him with a description of the coasts and thus of the shape and size of countries. Book VII was based on the same authorities and described the Danube Basin and the European coasts of the Black Sea. Writing about Greece, in books VIII to X, he still relied upon Artemidorus, but the bulk of his information was taken from two commentators of Homer—Apollodorus of Athens (2nd century BCE) and Demetrius of Scepsis (born around 205 BCE)—for Strabo placed great emphasis on identifying the cities named in the Greek epic the *Iliad*. Books XI to XIV describe the Asian shores of the Black Sea, the Caucasus, northern Iran, and Asia Minor. Here Strabo made the greatest use of his own observations, though he often quoted historians who dealt with the wars fought in these regions and cited Demetrius on problems of Homeric topography in the region about ancient Troy. India and Persia (Book XV) were described according to information given by the historians of the campaigns of Alexander the Great (356 to 323 BCE), whereas his descriptions of Mesopotamia, Syria, Palestine, and the Red Sea (Book XVI) were based on the accounts of the expeditions sent out by Mark Antony (about 83 to 30 BCE) and by the emperor Augustus, as well as on chapters on ethnography in Posidonius and on the book of a Red Sea voyage taken by the Greek historian and geographer Agatharchides (2nd century BCE). Strabo's own memories of Egypt, supplemented by the writings of Posidonius and Artemidorus, provided material for the substance of Book XVII, which dealt with the African shores of the Mediterranean Sea and with Mauretania.

Obviously, personal travel notes formed only a small part of the material used in this considerable work, although Strabo prided himself on having travelled westward from Armenia as far as the regions of Tuscany opposite Sardinia, and southward from the Black Sea as far as the frontiers of Ethiopia. Even on the subject of Italy, where he lived for a long time, Strabo did not himself contribute more than a few scattered impressions. His material, accordingly, mostly dates from the time of the sources he used, although the reader is not made aware of this. The value of firsthand observations, chosen from the sources with care, compensates, however, for his lack of originality and contemporaneousness. Strabo showed himself equally competent in selecting useful information—giving distances from city to city and mentioning the frontiers between countries or provinces as well as the main agricultural and industrial activities, political statutes, ethnographic peculiarities, and religious practices. He also took interest in the histories of cities and states, and—when he knew them—mentioned the circumstances under which they were founded, related myths or legends, wars they had instigated or endured, their expansion or recession, and their celebrities. Geological phenomena were reported when they were in some way unusual or when they furnished an explanation for other phenomena—such as the Atlantic tides in Iberia, the volcanic landscapes to be seen in southern Italy and Sicily, the fountains of naphtha occurring near the Euphrates River, and the rise and fall of the Nile waters. Paradoxically, although the description of Greece fills three whole books, such elements are virtually neglected in them. In this part, indeed, Strabo was more attracted by the problem of identifying the localities mentioned in Homer's works than in the geographical realities. These books, however, illustrate another side of his thought, based on the conviction that Homer was perfectly acquainted with the geography of the Mediterranean area and that the correct critical interpretation would reveal his vast learning. This classical thesis is abundantly defended in Strabo's introduction, which attacks the skepticism of Eratosthenes; moreover, it represents, in Strabo's work, the specific contribution to learning of the Greek cultural tradition.

WILLIAM THOMSON, BARON KELVIN

(b. June 26, 1824, Belfast, County Antrim, Ire. [now in Northern Ireland]—d. Dec. 17, 1907, Netherhall, near Largs, Ayrshire, Scot.)

Sir William Thompson, Baron Kelvin of Largs, was a Scottish engineer, mathematician, and physicist who profoundly influenced the scientific thought of his generation. Thomson, who was knighted and raised to the peerage in recognition of his work in engineering and physics, was foremost among the small group of British scientists who helped to lay the foundations of modern physics. His contributions to science included a major role in the development of the second law of thermodynamics; the absolute temperature scale (measured in kelvins); the dynamical theory of heat; the mathematical analysis of electricity and magnetism, including the basic ideas for the electromagnetic theory of light; the geophysical determination of the age of Earth; and fundamental work in hydrodynamics. His theoretical work on submarine telegraphy and his inventions for use on submarine cables aided Britain in capturing a preeminent place in world communication during the 19th century.

The style and character of Thomson's scientific and engineering work reflected his active personality. While a student at the University of Cambridge, he was awarded silver sculls for winning the university championship in racing single-seater rowing shells. He was an inveterate traveler all of his life, spending much time on the Continent and making several trips to the United States. In later life he commuted between homes in London and Glasgow. Thomson risked his life several times during the laying of the first transatlantic cable.

William Thomson, Baron Kelvin, oil painting by Elizabeth King, 1886–87; in the National Portrait Gallery, London. Courtesy of The National Portrait Gallery, London

Thomson's worldview was based in part on the belief that all phenomena that caused force—such as electricity, magnetism, and heat—were the result of invisible material in motion. This belief placed him in the forefront of those scientists who opposed the view that forces were produced by imponderable fluids. By the end of the century, however, Thomson, having persisted in his belief, found himself in opposition to the positivistic outlook that proved to be a prelude to 20th-century quantum mechanics and relativity. Consistency of worldview eventually placed him counter to the mainstream of science.

But Thomson's consistency enabled him to apply a few basic ideas to a number of areas of study. He brought together disparate areas of physics—heat, thermodynamics, mechanics, hydrodynamics, magnetism, and electricity—and thus played a principal role in the great and final synthesis of 19th-century science, which viewed all physical change as energy-related phenomena. Thomson was also the first to suggest that there were mathematical analogies between kinds of energy. His success as a synthesizer of theories about energy places him in the same position in 19th-century physics that Sir Isaac Newton has in 17th-century physics or Albert Einstein in 20th-century physics. All of these great synthesizers prepared the ground for the next grand leap forward in science.

EARLY LIFE

William Thomson was the fourth child in a family of seven. His mother died when he was six years old. His father, James Thomson, who was a textbook writer, taught mathematics, first in Belfast and later as a professor at the University of Glasgow; he taught his sons the most recent mathematics, much of which had not yet become a part of the British university curriculum. An unusually close relationship between a dominant father and a submissive son served to develop William's extraordinary mind.

William, age 10, and his brother James, age 11, matriculated at the University of Glasgow in 1834. There William was introduced to the advanced and controversial thinking of Jean-Baptiste-Joseph Fourier when one of Thomson's professors loaned him Fourier's pathbreaking book *The Analytical Theory of Heat*, which applied abstract mathematical techniques to the study of heat flow through any solid object. Thomson's first two published articles, which appeared when he was 16 and 17 years old, were a defense of Fourier's work, which was then under attack by British scientists. Thomson was the first to promote the idea that Fourier's mathematics, although applied solely to the flow of heat, could be used in the study of other forms of energy—whether fluids in motion or electricity flowing through a wire.

Thomson won many university awards at Glasgow, and at the age of 15 he won a gold medal for "An Essay on the Figure of the Earth," in which he exhibited exceptional mathematical ability. That essay, highly original in its analysis, served as a source of scientific ideas for Thomson throughout his life. He last consulted the essay just a few months before he died at the age of 83.

Thomson entered Cambridge in 1841 and took a B.A. degree four years later with high honours. In 1845 he was given a copy of George Green's *An Essay on the Application of Mathematical Analysis to the Theories of Electricity and Magnetism*. That work and Fourier's book were the components from which Thomson shaped his worldview and that helped him create his pioneering synthesis of the mathematical relationship between electricity and heat. After finishing at Cambridge, Thomson went to Paris, where he worked in the laboratory of the physicist and chemist Henri-Victor Regnault to gain practical experimental competence to supplement his theoretical education.

The chair of natural philosophy (later called physics) at the University of Glasgow fell vacant in 1846. Thomson's father then mounted a carefully planned and energetic campaign to have his son named to the position, and at the age of 22 William was unanimously elected to it.

Thomson's scientific work was guided by the conviction that the various theories dealing with matter and energy were converging toward one great, unified theory. He pursued the goal of a unified theory even though he doubted that it was attainable in his lifetime or ever. The basis for Thomson's conviction was the cumulative impression obtained from experiments showing the interrelation of forms of energy. By the middle of the 19th century it had been shown that magnetism and electricity, electromagnetism, and light were related, and Thomson had shown by mathematical analogy that there was a relationship between hydrodynamic phenomena and an electric current flowing through wires. James Prescott Joule also claimed that there was a relationship between mechanical motion and heat, and his idea became the basis for the science of thermodynamics.

In 1847, at a meeting of the British Association for the Advancement of Science, Thomson first heard Joule's theory about the interconvertibility of heat and motion. Joule's theory went counter to the accepted knowledge of the time, which was that heat was an imponderable substance (caloric) and could not be, as Joule claimed, a form of motion. Thomson was open-minded enough to discuss with Joule the implications of the new theory. At the time, though he could not accept Joule's idea, Thomson was willing to reserve judgment, especially since the relationship between heat and mechanical motion fit into his own view of the causes of force. By 1851 Thomson was able to give public recognition to Joule's theory, along with a cautious endorsement in a major mathematical treatise, "On the Dynamical Theory of Heat." Thomson's essay contained his version of the second law of thermodynamics, which was a major step toward the unification of scientific theories.

Thomson's work on electricity and magnetism also began during his student days at Cambridge. When, much

William Thomson, 1852. © Photos.com/Thinkstock

later, James Clerk Maxwell decided to undertake research in magnetism and electricity, he read all of Thomson's papers on the subject and adopted Thomson as his mentor. Maxwell—in his attempt to synthesize all that was known about the interrelationship of electricity, magnetism, and light—developed his monumental electromagnetic theory of light, probably the most significant achievement of 19th-century science. This theory had its genesis in Thomson's work, and Maxwell readily acknowledged his debt.

Thomson's contributions to 19th-century science were many. He advanced the ideas of Michael Faraday, Fourier, Joule, and others. Using mathematical analysis, Thomson drew generalizations from experimental results. He formulated the concept that was to be generalized into the dynamic theory of energy. He also collaborated with a number of leading scientists of the time, among them Sir George Gabriel Stokes, Hermann von Helmholtz, Peter Guthrie Tait, and Joule. With these partners, he advanced the frontiers of science in several areas, particularly hydrodynamics. Furthermore, Thomson originated the mathematical analogy between the flow of heat in solid bodies and the flow of electricity in conductors.

Thomson's involvement in a controversy over the feasibility of laying a transatlantic cable changed the course of his professional work. His work on the project began in 1854 when Stokes, a lifelong correspondent on scientific matters, asked for a theoretical explanation of the apparent delay in an electric current passing through a long cable. In his reply, Thomson referred to his early paper "On the Uniform Motion of Heat in Homogeneous Solid Bodies, and its Connexion with the Mathematical Theory of Electricity" (1842). Thomson's idea about the mathematical analogy between heat flow and electric current worked well in his analysis of the problem of sending telegraph messages through the planned 3,000-mile (4,800-km) cable. His equations describing the flow of heat through a solid wire proved applicable to questions about the velocity of a current in a cable.

The publication of Thomson's reply to Stokes prompted a rebuttal by E.O.W. Whitehouse, the Atlantic Telegraph Company's chief electrician. Whitehouse claimed that practical experience refuted Thomson's theoretical findings, and for a time Whitehouse's view prevailed with the directors of the company. Despite their disagreement, Thomson participated, as chief consultant, in the hazardous early cable-laying expeditions. In 1858 Thomson patented his telegraph receiver, called a mirror galvanometer, for use on the Atlantic cable. (The device, along with his later modification called the siphon recorder, came to be used on most of the worldwide network of submarine cables.) Eventually the directors of the Atlantic Telegraph Company fired Whitehouse, adopted Thomson's suggestions for the design of the cable, and decided in favour of the mirror galvanometer. Thomson was knighted in 1866 by Queen Victoria for his work.

LATER LIFE

After the successful laying of the transatlantic cable, Thomson became a partner in two engineering consulting firms, which played a major role in the planning and construction of submarine cables during the frenzied era of expansion that resulted in a global network of telegraph communication. Thomson became a wealthy man who could afford a 126-ton yacht and a baronial estate.

Thomson's interests in science included not only electricity, magnetism, thermodynamics, and hydrodynamics but also geophysical questions about tides, the shape of Earth, atmospheric electricity, thermal studies of the ground, Earth's rotation, and geomagnetism. He also entered the controversy over Charles Darwin's theory of evolution. Thomson opposed Darwin, remaining "on the side of the angels."

Thomson challenged the views on geologic and biological change of the early uniformitarians, including Darwin, who claimed that Earth and its life had evolved over an incalculable number of years, during which the forces of nature always operated as at present. On the basis of thermodynamic theory and Fourier's studies, Thomson in 1862 estimated that more than one million years ago the Sun's heat and Earth's temperature must have been considerably greater and that these conditions had produced violent storms and floods and an entirely different type of vegetation. His views, published in 1868, particularly

angered Darwin's support-
ers. Thomas Henry Huxley
replied to Thomson in
the 1869 Anniversary
Address of the President
of the Geological Society
of London. Thomson's
speculations as to the age
of Earth and the Sun were
inaccurate, but he did
succeed in pressing his
contention that biological
and geologic theory had to
conform to the well-estab-
lished theories of physics.

In an 1884 series of
lectures at Johns Hopkins
University on the state
of scientific knowledge,
Thomson wondered aloud

William Thomson, Baron Kelvin, with his compass, 1902. © Photos .com/Thinkstock

about the failures of the wave theory of light to explain
certain phenomena. His interest in the sea, roused aboard
his yacht, the *Lalla Rookh*, resulted in a number of patents:
a compass that was adopted by the British Admiralty; a
form of analog computer for measuring tides in a harbour
and for calculating tide tables for any hour, past or future;
and sounding equipment. He established a company to
manufacture these items and a number of electrical measuring devices. Like his father, he published a textbook,
Treatise on Natural Philosophy (1867), a work on physics
coauthored with Tait that helped shape the thinking of a
generation of physicists.

Despite blandishments from Cambridge, Thomson
had remained at the University of Glasgow for the entirety
of his career. He resigned his university chair in 1899, at

William Thomson, Baron Kelvin, delivering his last lecture at the University of Glasgow, 1899. © Photos.com/Thinkstock

the age of 75, after 53 years of a fruitful and happy association with the institution. He was making room, he said, for younger men.

Thomson was said to be entitled to more letters after his name than any other man in the Commonwealth. He received honorary degrees from universities throughout the world and was lauded by engineering societies and scientific organizations. He was elected a fellow of the Royal Society in 1851 and served as its president from 1890 to 1895. He published more than 600 papers and was granted dozens of patents. He died at his estate in Scotland and was buried in Westminster Abbey, London.

ALFRED LOTHAR WEGENER

(b. Nov. 1, 1880, Berlin, Ger.—d. November 1930, Greenland)

German meteorologist and geophysicist Alfred Wegener formulated the first complete statement of the continental drift hypothesis. The son of an orphanage director, Wegener earned a Ph.D. degree in astronomy from the University of Berlin in 1905. He had meanwhile become interested in paleoclimatology, and in 1906–08 he took part in an expedition to Greenland to study polar air circulation. He made three more expeditions to Greenland, in 1912–13, 1929, and 1930. He taught meteorology at Marburg and Hamburg and was a professor of meteorology and geophysics at the University of Graz from 1924 to 1930. He died during his last expedition to Greenland in 1930.

Like certain other scientists before him, Wegener became impressed with the similarity in the coastlines of eastern South America and western Africa and speculated that those lands had once been joined together. In about 1910 he began toying with the idea that in the Late Paleozoic era (about 250 million years ago) all the present-day continents had formed a single large mass, or supercontinent, which had subsequently broken apart. Wegener called this ancient continent Pangaea. Other scientists had proposed such a continent but had explained the separation of the modern world's continents as having resulted from the subsidence, or sinking, of large portions of the supercontinent to form the Atlantic and Indian oceans. Wegener, by contrast, proposed that Pangaea's constituent portions had slowly moved thousands of miles apart over long periods of geologic time. His term for this movement was *die*

Alfred Lothar Wegener. Photos.com/ Jupiter Images

Verschiebung der Kontinente ("continental displacement"), which gave rise to the term continental drift.

Wegener first presented his theory in lectures in 1912 and published it in full in 1915 in his most important work, *Die Entstehung der Kontinente und Ozeane* (*The Origin of Continents and Oceans*). He searched the scientific literature for geological and paleontological evidence that would buttress his theory, and he was able to point to many closely related fossil organisms and similar rock strata that occurred on widely separated continents, particularly those found in both the Americas and in Africa. Wegener's theory of continental drift won some adherents in the ensuing decade, but his postulations of the driving forces behind the continents' movement seemed implausible. By 1930 his theory had been rejected by most geologists, and it sank into obscurity for the next few decades, only to be resurrected as part of the theory of plate tectonics (*q.v.*) during the 1960s.

ABRAHAM GOTTLOB WERNER

(b. Sept. 25, 1750, Wehrau, Saxony—d. June 30, 1817, Freiberg)

German geologist Abraham Gottlob Werner founded the Neptunist school, which proclaimed the aqueous origin of all rocks, in opposition to the Plutonists, or Vulcanists, who argued that granite and many other rocks were of igneous origin. Werner rejected uniformitarianism (belief that geological evolution has been a uniform and continuous process).

A member of an old iron-mining family, Werner worked with his father for five years in the ironworks at Wehrau and Lorzendorf. In 1775 he was appointed inspector and teacher in the Freiburg School of Mining. During his 40-year tenure, the school grew from a local academy into a world-renowned centre of scientific learning. Werner was a brilliant lecturer and a man of great charm, and his genius attracted students who, inspired by him, became the foremost geologists of Europe.

A distinguishing feature of Werner's teaching was the care with which he taught the study of rocks and minerals and the orderly succession of geological formations, a subject that he called geognosy. Influenced by the works of Johann Gottlob Lehmann and Georg Christian Füchsel, Werner demonstrated that the rocks of Earth are deposited in a definite order. Although he had never travelled, he assumed that the sequence of the rocks he observed in Saxony was the same for the rest of the world. He believed that Earth was once completely covered by the oceans and that, with time, all the minerals were precipitated out of the water into distinct layers, a theory known as Neptunism.

Because this theory did not allow for a molten core, he proposed that volcanoes were recent phenomena caused by the spontaneous combustion of underground coal beds. He asserted that basalt and similar rocks were accumulations of the ancient ocean, whereas other geologists recognized them as igneous minerals. It was primarily disagreement on this point that formed one of the great geological controversies.

Werner wrote only 26 scientific works, most of them short contributions to journals. His aversion to writing grew, and finally he adopted the practice of storing his mail unopened. Elected a foreign member of the Académie des Sciences in 1812, he learned of the honour much later, when he happened to read about it in a journal. In spite of his failure to produce extensive geological writings, Werner's theories were faithfully adopted and widely spread by his loyal students. Even though many of them eventually discarded his Neptunist theories, they would not publicly renounce them while Werner still lived.

GLOSSARY

brachiopods Marine animals, such as clams, which have two symmetric shells and tentacles or "arms" used to gather food.

diagenesis The chemical process by which sediment becomes rock.

geoid A model of Earth that coincides with sea level, and serves as a reference from which to gauge topographic heights and ocean depths.

geologic age A period of time as determined by major geological events.

gravimetric Of or relating to variations in the gravitational field.

igneous Any of various crystalline or glassy, noncrystalline rocks formed by the cooling and solidification of molten magma.

magma Molten or partially molten rock consisting primarily of silicate liquid from Earth's core.

metamorphic Any of a class of rocks that result from the alteration of preexisting rocks in response to changing geological conditions, including variations in temperature, pressure, and mechanical stress.

mineralogy The scientific discipline concerned with all aspects of minerals, including their physical properties, chemical composition, internal crystal structure, and occurrence and distribution in nature.

paleontology The science wherein periods along the geologic scale are studied.

petrology The science that deals with the origin, history, occurrence, structure, chemical composition, and classification of rocks.

pyroclastic Formed by or involving fragmentation as a result of volcanic or igneous action.

resistivity The longitudinal electrical resistance of a uniform rod of unit length and unit cross-sectional area.

sedimentary A type of rock formed by or from deposits of sediment.

sondes Any of various devices for testing physical conditions, particularly at high altitudes or below Earth's surface.

spectrometer An analytical instrument used to measure the dispersion of an emission, such as radiation.

strata In geology, a sheetlike mass of sedimentary rock or earth of one kind lying between beds of other kinds.

subduction The action or process in plate tectonics of the edge of one crustal plate descending below the edge of another.

subterranean Existing or operating beneath Earth's surface.

uniformitarianism In geology, the doctrine that existing processes acting in the same manner and with essentially the same intensity as at present are sufficient to account for all geologic change.

BIBLIOGRAPHY

GEOLOGY

Popular introductions include Preston Cloud, *Oasis in Space: Earth History from the Beginning* (1988), a very readable account written for the general public; and Frank Press et al., *Understanding Earth*, 4th ed. (2003), a beautifully illustrated popular introduction to geology. Other readable general accounts are Eldridge M. Moores (ed.), *Shaping the Earth: Tectonics of Continents and Oceans: Readings from Scientific American Magazine* (1990), a collection of well-illustrated papers on plate tectonics and mountain building; Brian J. Skinner, Stephen C. Porter, and Jeffrey Park, *Dynamic Earth: An Introduction to Physical Geology*, 5th ed. (2004), a well-illustrated introduction to geology; and Kent C. Condie, *Plate Tectonics and Crustal Evolution*, 4th ed. (1997), an advanced but accessible account of the origin and development of Earth's crust. Notable encyclopaedias in the geological sciences include Philip Kearey (ed.), *The Encyclopedia of the Solid Earth Sciences* (1993), a very useful definition of almost everything geological; and Eldridge M. Moores and Rhodes W. Fairbridge, *Encyclopedia of European and Asian Regional Geology* (1997). Additional modern treatments of physical geology are provided in Edward J. Tarbuck, Frederick K. Lutgens, and Dennis Tasa, *Earth: An Introduction to Physical Geology*, 10th ed. (2010); Charles Plummer and Diane Carlson, *Physical Geology*, 13th ed. (2009); and Gary A. Smith and Aurora Pun, *How Does Earth Work? Physical Geology and the Process of Science*, 2nd ed. (2009).

EARTH STRUCTURE AND SURFACE FEATURES

Coverage of the composition, structure, and surface features of Earth is provided in Eldridge M. Moores and Robert J. Twiss, *Tectonics* (1995), a comprehensive treatment of all tectonic environments; P.McL.D. Duff, *Holmes' Principles of Physical Geology*, 4th ed. (1993), a thorough and stimulating coverage of physical geology; Marjorie Wilson, *Igneous Petrogenesis* (1989, reissued 1996), a work relating igneous geology to plate tectonics; and G.C. Brown and A.E. Mussett, *The Inaccessible Earth*, 2nd ed. (1993), a readable treatment of the geophysics of Earth's core, mantle, and crust.

Volcanism, seismicity, and their relationship to plate tectonics are studied in Peter Francis and Clive Oppenheimer, *Volcanoes*, 2nd ed. (2004); David Chester, *Volcanoes and Society* (1993), a general treatment of the impact of volcanoes on society today; Robert S. Yeats, Kerry Sieh, and Clarence R. Allen, *The Geology of Earthquakes* (1997), a work that outlines the relationships between earthquake geophysics and geological environments; Bruce A. Bolt, *Earthquakes*, 5th ed. (2003), a good introduction to the whole field; Edward A. Keller and Nicholas Pinter, *Active Tectonics: Earthquakes, Uplift, and Landscape*, 2nd ed. (2002), a stimulating overview; and Michael A. Summerfield (ed.), *Geomorphology and Global Tectonics* (2000), a comprehensive synthesis of landforms and landscapes.

EARTH HISTORY AND ASTROGEOLOGY

Historical geology is treated in William K. Hartmann, *The History of Earth: An Illustrated Chronicle of an Evolving Planet* (1991), a beautifully illustrated introduction; and Brian F.

Windley, *The Evolving Continents*, 3rd ed. (1995), a detailed, comprehensive synthesis of evidence related to continental evolution throughout geologic time. Gary Nichols, *Sedimentology and Stratigraphy* (1999), provides a modern introduction to the deposition of sediments. Felix M. Gradstein, James G. Ogg, and Alan G. Smith, *A Geologic Time Scale 2004* (2004), is one of the premier works of modern stratigraphy. Paleontology is considered in Michael J. Benton, *Vertebrate Palaeontology*, 3rd ed. (2005), a treatment of the history of vertebrate evolution from the early fishes to the dinosaurs; and J. William Schopf, *Cradle of Life: The Discovery of Earth's Earliest Fossils* (1999), an entertaining and informative book on early life on Earth. Astrogeology is described in Eric A.K. Middlemost, *Magmas, Rocks, and Planetary Development* (1997), a work that puts terrestrial igneous rocks into a planetary perspective; and Ronald Greeley, *Planetary Landscapes*, 2nd ed. (1994), a treatment combining abundant photos of the planets and their satellites with text explaining their geomorphology and geology.

PRACTICAL APPLICATIONS OF GEOLOGY

Applied works include M. Vaněček (ed.), *Mineral Deposits of the World: Ores, Industrial Minerals, and Rocks* (1994), a useful synthesis of economic geology; Peter W. Harben and Milŏs Kužvart, *Industrial Minerals: A Global Geology* (1997), a treatment covering all the main minerals used in industry; Dorothy J. Merritts, Andrew De Wet, and Kirsten Menking, *Environmental Geology: An Earth System Science Approach* (1998), a well-illustrated overview of the subject; and Kevin T. Pickering and Lewis A. Owen, *An Introduction to Global Environmental Issues*, 2nd ed. (1997), a popular treatment of the environmental problems affecting society today.

EARTH SCIENCES

Textbook treatments of the Earth sciences are provided in Edward J. Tarbuck, Frederick K. Lutgens, and Dennis Tasa, *Earth Science*, 12th ed. (2008); Stephen Marshak, *Earth: Portait of a Planet*, 3rd ed. (2007); and Frederick K. Lutgens, Edward J. Tarbuck, and Dennis Tasa, *Foundations of Earth Science*, 5th ed. (2007).

The history of the Earth sciences is recounted in Henry Faul and Carol Faul, *It Began with a Stone: A History of Geology from the Stone Age to the Age of Plate Tectonics* (1983); Mott T. Greene, *Geology in the Nineteenth Century: Changing Views on a Changing World* (1982), a history of tectonic thinking concerned with the formation of mountains and earth evolution; A. Hallam, *Great Geological Controversies* (1983), an evaluation of celebrated controversies from Neptunism to continental drift; Robert Muir Wood, *The Dark Side of the Earth: The Battle for the Earth Sciences, 1800–1980* (1985), a history of important controversies; Rachel Laudan, *From Mineralogy to Geology: The Foundations of a Science, 1650-1830* (1987), which traces the intellectual roots of geology to mineralogy and chemical cosmogony; Stephen Toulmin and June Goodfield, *The Discovery of Time* (1965, reprinted 1983), which traces the history of the idea of geologic time; William Whewell, *History of the Inductive Sciences from the Earliest to the Present Time*, 3rd ed., 3 vol. (1857, reissued 1976)—vol. 2 containing an analysis of uniformitarian and catastrophist views of Earth history; and Karl Alfred Von Zittel, *History of Geology and Palaeontology to the End of the Nineteenth Century* (1901, reissued 1962; originally published in German, 1899, reprinted 1965), best for its history of paleontology.

Modern treatments of paleontology include Michael Foote and Arnold I. Miller, *Paleontology* 3rd ed. (2006); Harold L. Levin, *The Earth Through Time*, 9th ed. (2009); and Morris S. Petersen and J. Keith Rigby, *Interpreting Earth History: A Manual in Historical Geology*, 6th ed. (2008).

EARTH EXPLORATION

Texts on methodology and discoveries in Earth exploration include C.M.R. Fowler, *The Solid Earth: An Introduction to Global Geophysics*, 2nd ed. (2005); P.V. Sharma, *Geophysical Methods in Geology*, 2nd ed. (1986); William Lowrie, *Fundamentals in Geophysics*, 2nd ed. (2007); R.E. Sheriff and L.P. Geldart, *Exploration Seismology*, 2nd ed. (1995); Philip Kearey, Michael Brooks, and Ian Hill, *An Introduction to Geophysical Exploration*, 3rd ed. (2002); Robert F. Butler, *Paleomagnetism: Magnetic Domains to Geologic Terranes* (1992); J.D.A. Piper, *Palaeomagnetism and the Continental Crust* (1987); Willliam C. Peters, *Exploration and Mining Geology*, 2nd ed. (1987); Floyd F. Sabins, *Remote Sensing: Principles and Interpretation*, 3rd ed. (1997); and R.E. Sheriff (compiler), *Encyclopedic Dictionary of Exploration Geophysics*, 3rd ed. (1991).

INDEX